LIVING WATERS

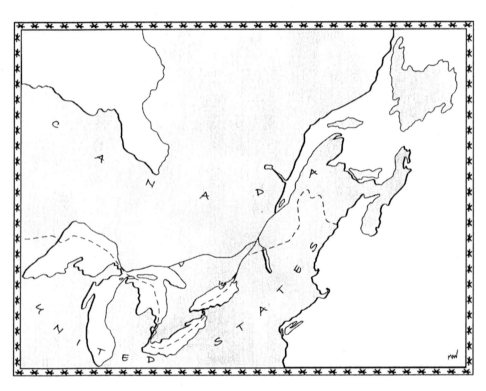

THE GREAT LAKES—ST. LAWRENCE RIVER SYSTEM

MARGARET WOOSTER

LIVING WATERS

Reading the Rivers of the Lower Great Lakes

excelsior editions

State University of New York Press
Albany, New York

Published by
STATE UNIVERSITY OF NEW YORK PRESS, ALBANY

© 2009 State University of New York

For information, contact State University of New York Press
www.sunypress.edu

Production and book design, Laurie D. Searl
Marketing, Susan M. Petrie

Library of Congress Cataloging in Publication Data

Wooster, Margaret.
  Living waters : reading the rivers of the lower Great Lakes / Mar-
garet Wooster.
      p. cm.
  Includes bibliographical references and index.
  ISBN 978-0-7914-7703-8 (hardcover : alk. paper)
  ISBN 978-0-7914-7704-5 (pbk. : alk. paper) 1. Great Lakes
Region (North America)—Environmental conditions. 2. Water-
supply—Great Lakes Region (North America) 3. Ecology—Great
Lakes Region (North America) 4. Great Lakes Region (North
America)—Description and travel. I. Title.
  GE160.G75W66 2009
  333.91'620977—dc22

                                                    2008017299

10 9 8 7 6 5 4 3 2

CONTENTS

CONTENTS

ILLUSTRATIONS

ACKNOWLEDGEMENTS

I am grateful to Buffalo Niagara Riverkeeper, Great Lakes United, the Erie and Niagara Counties Regional Planning Board, and the SUNY Buffalo School of Architecture and Planning for providing the opportunities to study, map and otherwise explore many of these rivers and their watersheds.

I also want to thank readers Ray Vaughan, Neil Patterson, Carl Dennis, Lynda Schneekloth and Kathleen Marien; fellow travelers Neil Schmitz, Maureen Wall, Taylor Schmitz, and Suzanne Simon; and early guides now gone but not forgotten: Twylah Nitsch, founder of the Seneca Nation Historical Society, David Bigelow, naturalist and educator for the Buffalo Museum of Science, and my parents, Gregory and Evelyn Wooster, life-long practitioners of Baha'i principles, especially the "independent investigation of truth."

Dave Dempsey, Great Lakes author and advocate, encouraged me to see the book through and helped me to shift my focus from the agendas we brought to Washington DC and Ottawa, to the experiences that made me care in the first place.

Nellie Schmitz, creative director and owner of NextLevel Communications, digitized and edited my maps and photographs with great skill and sensitivity. She also introduced me to the Leopold Legacy Center in Baraboo Wisconsin, once a dustbowl farm Aldo Leopold bought for "its lack of goodness," now a state-of-the-art resource for ecological restoration and sustainable design.

Western New York Heritage Press published an earlier version of Chapter 5, "Genesee Torture Tree: Rereading Little Beard's Signs" in the Spring 2005 edition of *Western New York Heritage Magazine*. Many thanks also to the following people and institutions who provided images for this book: the Buffalo Museum of Science; Buffalo and Erie County Historical Society; Butler Library *Courier Express* archive at Buffalo State College; Historic Urban Plans, Inc., Ithaca NY; Holland Land Company Office Museum, Batavia NY; NASA Johnson Space Center; Niagara Falls NY Public Library, Local History Department; *Niagara Gazette*; PVS Chemical Solutions, Inc.; University of California Press; U.S. Geological Survey/EROS; Kathy McGoldrick and Maureen Wall.

FOREWORD

STANDING AT THE TIP of Lookout Point 300 feet above Cattaraugus Creek, I can just make out the elongated entrance to a cave across the valley, high in the canyon's north wall. I have spent years tracking down this cave—not because I wanted to explore it, but because I needed to confirm its existence. Locally known as "the Indian Cave," this hole-in-the-wall is the epicenter for a collection of cultural, ethical, and geological interpretations of the landscape that, taken together, could serve as the eastern Great Lakes region's own Book of Genesis. It is good to know that, even though my perch may soon be sacrificed to the powerful erosive forces that continue to downcut this valley, the cave is still there.

This book is based on the premise that the first step toward becoming responsible tenants of the Great Lakes bioregion—the world's largest freshwater ecosystem—is to render that enormous abstraction into something, as Aldo Leopold says, "we can see, feel, understand, love, or otherwise have faith in."[1] Like the creation narrative lodged in that riverbank cave. My primary sources are the waters I know best across New York State and southern Québec. Specifically, from west to east, these are: Cattaraugus Creek, the Buffalo River, Scajaquada Creek, the Niagara, Genesee, and Oswego rivers, the ponds and brooks of the Adirondack highlands, and the majestic St. Lawrence making its 750-mile run to the sea. These waters tell many stories. They show why the native trout are disappearing and the eagles are coming back. They point out what we have in common with the whales in the St. Lawrence estuary. They demonstrate how the health of Lakes Erie and Ontario continues to deteriorate, but also how that decline could be reversed. They intimate what is going on underground.

Most of New York's big rivers and its two Great Lakes bear Indian names providing links to a deep cultural heritage. Iroquois or

Haudenosaunee[2] communities living on or near these rivers today are fighting and refighting battles to protect and restore them. I seek guidance in my river interpretations from Haudenosaunee colleagues across the state, many actively engaged in preserving and restoring traditional ecological knowledge.

I read rivers with a reinhabitation motive along the lines of conservationists like Aldo Leopold, agronomists like Wendell Berry and Wes Jackson, and bioregionalists like Peter Berg in their common project of "becoming native to this place." Like them, I think the more intimately we know the places in which we live, in all their natural and cultural particularity, the better equipped we will be to codesign healthy, sustainable communities for present and future generations.

Leopold has the last word. The final chapter measures our current Great Lakes water policies against the gold standard of his 1949 conservation ethic, a set of principles still more often quoted than applied.

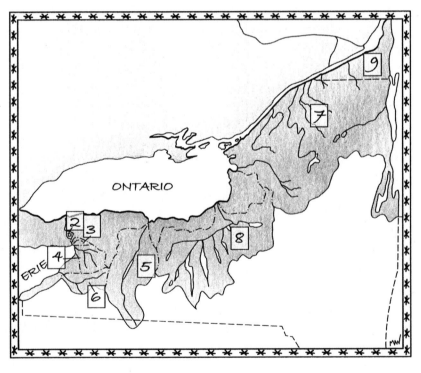

NEW YORK'S GREAT LAKES WATERSHEDS BY CHAPTER NUMBER

ONE

THE GLOBAL CONTEXT

In water, two hydrogen atoms always rest against the atom of oxygen at a 104.5 degree angle. This has been called the angle of life. This is the secret of why this is not a frozen, bleak planet.

—John Todd, 1990 inaugural address,
Center for the Restoration of Waters

GOT WATER?

As I WRITE THIS, I'm sipping a glass of water. Eight glasses a day is my goal, beginning with the first glass every morning to break the fast of sleep and pump things up enough to handle the coming slug of strong black coffee. We humans, as someone on *Star Trek* once said, "are bags of mostly water." Water makes up over 60 percent of our bodies and 70 percent of our brains. Babies are 90 percent water.

In ice or liquid form, water covers about 70 percent of the earth's surface. But for the purposes of this book I am interested in less than 1 percent of that water—the tiny portion that is fresh and readily available for human use.

The United Nations World Water Assessment Program estimates that one in six people, or a little over one billion people, currently lack access to adequate drinking water. They forecast that at least one in four people will be living in countries with serious water shortages by 2050 if the world keeps consuming water at today's rates. That outlook may be conservative since, in the 1990s alone, per capita water consumption on the planet rose at about twice the rate of population growth. This trend in increased water use is not necessarily due to you or me taking more baths. It factors in global industrialization, including massive irrigation for industrialized farming, which accounts for up to 80 percent of our planet's water use.[1]

The report also raises many questions about the *quality* of our future water. Will it pass even our most basic measures? Will it be drinkable? Fishable? Swimmable? Over half the world's lakes and estuaries are now too contaminated for fishing or swimming. Their systems for recharge and recovery have been compromised by the cutting of neighboring forests, the filling of wetlands and floodplains, and the discharge and accumulation of human and industrial wastes. Drinking from these sources may still be possible thanks to chemical treatment, primarily chlorination. But chlorination adds problems of its own, and only disinfects water for those who can get it from a pipe, which excludes a large portion of humanity and all other species that depend on raw water supplies.

MOST OF US KNOW comparatively little about the natural processes that sustain Earth's creeks, rivers, lakes, and groundwater. Most of us think someone else is minding the water. Based on my own explorations of Great Lakes waters, I'd say this is a dangerous delusion.

Within the last two decades, research on aquatic ecosystems such as that published by the Flathead Lake Biological Station at the University of Montana challenges our most basic views of how rivers work—though it remains relatively unknown to the engineers in charge of our waterways. These studies reveal that every stream is actually two interacting waterbodies: one above ground and one below. The groundwater does all the invisible housework of cleaning and providing storage, recharge, and nutrients to the waters above. Groundwater systems, called hyporheic or "below the flow" zones, also serve as a refuge for creatures during all or parts of their life cycle and assist in stream and species recovery after floods or droughts. Many previously unknown species of worms, shrimp, insects, and microscopic organisms were found below the flow, supporting a food chain that extends to the surface and beyond. Hyporheic zones have been measured as deep as 30 feet below streambeds and for miles on each side.[2]

Remember this the next time someone proposes putting your local creek or river in a concrete channel for flood control or in an underground culvert to accommodate development. Though the operation may be a success, the health of that stream and all who depend on it will suffer.

CONSIDER THE WATER that comes out of your tap. How did it cycle through its natural habitat? Where does it come from? Where does it go?

A light snow is drifting past my window this late January afternoon in Buffalo. Fallen snow is blowing down off the roofs and floating up from the driveway, big flakes up to an inch in diameter. Positioned as we are in the snow shadow of Lake Erie, we Buffalonians recognize this phenomenon as "snow flurries," meaning "intermittent snow with little or no accumulation," as opposed to "snow showers" (steady downfall), "snow squalls" (add wind), or "blizzard" (snow squalls and high winds sustained for at least—anything less is for wusses—three hours).

But what do we know about the role of snow in the water cycle? Specifically, how does the transformation to or from snow affect water?

Snowflakes are collections of individual ice crystals like the ones now stuck to my storm window. My snowflake field guide says the largest snowflake ever found was 8 by 12 inches, recorded in 1971 in Bratsk, Siberia. It must have contained millions of the tiny crystalline structures I can see clearly on my windowpane, which all look to me like variations on a six-pointed star. My guide identifies eight principal types of snow crystal: stellar dendrites, sectored plates, hollow columns, needles, spatial dendrites, capped columns, irregular crystals, and rimed crystals. Rene Descartes, sometimes called "the father of modern philosophy," began this snow crystal morphology in 1635. For some reason—perhaps it seemed a frivolous sideline to the heady enterprise of mind–body dualism—the work was not completed until over three hundred years later, when Ukichiro Nakaya published his exhaustive study, *Snow Crystals*, in 1950.

Besides being beautiful, what do these crystal structures do? Masaru Emoto, a practitioner of alternative medicine in Kyoto, Japan, studies water's variable ability to form crystals in connection with theories

1.1. SNOW CRYSTAL PHOTOGRAPHS BY WILSON A. BENT-
LEY. COURTESY OF THE BUFFALO MUSEUM OF SCIENCE.

concerning the healing properties of water. His research involves freez-
ing specimens of water from various sources, and then observing these
frozen drops of water under a microscope as they first begin to liquefy,
a process he has captured on film. Some water samples, like those from
the springs on Mount Fuji, form simple to elaborate hexagonal crystals.
Others, including samples of urban tap water from Tokyo, Paris, and
other cities around the world, do not. Emoto believes that the crystal-
forming power of water reveals its life energy or "hado," a centuries-old
Japanese word literally meaning "vibration." The absence of crystal-

forming ability indicates that the purity of that water source, and thus its ability to support life, is compromised.[3] Core to his healing practice is the belief that the life force of water can be restored through positive energy. In a lecture he has taken to cities around the world, he shows films of corrupted water samples regaining their crystal-forming ability after being exposed to music and prayer.

I may be too hopelessly Cartesian to be entirely comfortable with Emoto's conflation of mind and matter in these healing intricacies of water, but I am intrigued by his basic findings relating structural capabilities with different levels of purity. Is it possible that snow as a process in the hydrologic cycle not only reveals an atomic property of water but also helps restore it in some way, for example, by isolating or neutralizing impurities? Could the atmospheric cycling of water be as important to water's quality, its ability to support life, as the subsurface cycling through soil, sand, and rock?

If, from 5 miles up in an airplane you watch the rivers below, you might deduce that every stream is actually *three* interacting waterbodies: one working invisibly below the flow, one the glimmering flow of surface water, and one, often the only one you can see, the vapor cloud floating directly over the river, mirroring its sinuous curves, doing whatever work it is doing.

THE STATE OF THE GREAT LAKES

THOSE FORTY MILLION of us residing in the Great Lakes basin have a living laboratory in which to explore the mysteries of the water cycle. We are part of the largest freshwater ecosystem on earth, a system containing almost 20 percent of the world's fresh surface water.

Our earliest childhood lessons should lay the groundwork for appreciating this awesome fact. Where did all this freshwater come from? Why is it here?

The 5,500-cubic-mile deposit of water in the Great Lakes is a legacy of the glaciers, meltwater from the mile-thick layers of snow and ice that covered the region. The basin itself predates the glaciers by millions of years, its stratified foundation laid down by the great, shallow saltwater seas that intermittently covered much of the interior of what is now North America. Remnants of these seas and their different ecologies are everywhere to be found—from the fossilized corals and shells in the cliffs of Lake Erie, to the salt vein that is mined from a thousand feet below the Genesee River and redistributed over the ice and snow that reclaim the streets every winter.

The freshwater that now fills the Great Lakes basin is, like Saudi Arabia's oil, a limited supply. Geologists describe the Great Lakes as a relatively closed hydrologic system, with less than 1 percent of the water escaping annually through the St. Lawrence River to the sea, and less than 1 percent new water coming in from other watersheds in the form of rain or snow. That means that 99 percent of the water in the Great Lakes has been recirculating for 12,000 years through cycles of evaporation, precipitation, collection in wetlands and mountain ponds, runoff from cities, highways, farm fields, and eventual recharge back to the lakes.

This long retention capacity makes life in the Great Lakes vulnerable to contaminants that persist in the environment. In many ways, the planet's understanding of the connections between certain toxins in the environment and certain risks to organisms developed right here, in the Great Lakes region, though it took big signs—burning rivers, beaches covered with dead fish and rotting algae—to gain our attention.

I remember as a child helping my dad unload construction debris at one or another of Buffalo's waterfront dumps and I can attest to the fact that, on the industrialized shores of eastern Lake Erie and the Niagara River at least, we *expected* the waterfront to be burning and stinking and shrouded in smoke. It signaled, if not prosperity, then at least that people were working and that we belonged to some kind of economy.

But, in the 1970s, people began making the connection between human health, wildlife health, and water quality. Scientists traced the collapse of top predator wildlife populations like the bald eagle to eggshell thinning and other subtle failures in the reproductive cycle caused by DDT accumulated in Great Lakes fish. The cluster of illnesses afflicting an entire Niagara Falls neighborhood, especially the children, would soon be linked to the chemicals seeping through the groundwater at Love Canal. Something bad was happening on a major scale in the Great Lakes.

In response, in 1972, Canada and the United States signed the Great Lakes Water Quality Agreement, first to reduce phosphorous, the most obvious pollutant that had contributed to a "dead" or oxygen-poor Lake Erie, and then, as amended in 1978, to take on industrial contaminants, or "persistent toxic substances." The new objective of the federal, state, and provincial governments surrounding the Great Lakes was that "the discharge of toxic substances in toxic amounts be prohibited and the discharge of any or all persistent toxic substances be virtually eliminated."[4]

The first part of this much-examined sentence explains the regulatory regime we currently live under, as defined by the Clean Water Act in the United States and the Canadian Environmental Protection Act in Canada. States and provinces control industrial toxic releases by issuing permits whose thresholds are based, theoretically, on what the receiving water can safely dilute to some point of harmlessness.

The second part of the sentence designates the more radical approach of "virtual elimination" for *persistent* toxins, substances like mercury that live long and accumulate in animals. It commits both countries not only to eliminating discharges of the most toxic and bioaccumulative chemicals and metals (beginning with a list of the top twenty-two known to be harming Great Lakes fish and wildlife), but also to cleaning up forty-three "Areas of Concern"—highly contaminated rivers and harbors across the basin.

The International Joint Commission (IJC), created by the 1909 Boundary Waters Treaty to assist Canada and the Unites States in the protection of the lakes and rivers we hold in common, became the official watchdog to ensure the implementation of these commitments. In their 1992 *Sixth Biennial Report on Great Lakes Water Quality*, the IJC drove home the urgency for ridding the Great Lakes of persistent toxic substances:

> Because persistent toxic substances remain in the environment for long periods of time and become widely dispersed, and because they bioaccumulate in plants and animals—including humans—that make up the food web, the ecosystem cannot assimilate these substances. We conclude that persistent toxic substances are too dangerous to the biosphere and to humans to permit their release in *any* quantity . . . Zero discharge means just that: halting all inputs from human sources and pathways to prevent any opportunity for persistent toxic substances to enter

the environment as a result of human activity. To prevent such releases completely, their manufacture, use, transport and disposal must stop; they simply must not be available.[5]

How are we doing on these commitments?

Every two years since 1994, researchers from both countries issue a report on the health of the Great Lakes. One important measure is the amount of mercury, PCBs (polychlorinated biphenyls), dioxin, and other persistent toxins found in the fish from each lake. Since sampling began, levels have dropped but remain high enough to necessitate government advisories throughout the Great Lakes and their tributaries limiting the amount of fish people can safely consume. Women and children are especially at risk due to the interference of these substances with hormones that determine fetal and child development. We owe much of our understanding of how environmental toxins threaten human and animal health to the work of Dr. Theo Colborn. Her groundbreaking collaborative research showed how PCBs and other chlorinated compounds in the fat of fish-eating mothers are transferred to the developing young (in egg or womb). There, depending on dose and timing, they can interrupt normal development to cause an array of ills, from reproductive failures and physical deformities in bald eagles and beluga whales, to long-term immune system impairments and learning deficits in humans.[6]

But haven't we had dramatic reductions in toxic discharges over the past thirty years? Why are they still showing up in Great Lakes animals?

There are at least two answers to these questions.

First, although some contaminants have been greatly reduced, the Clean Water Act goal of eliminating all pollutants to all waters of the United States by 1985 remains a distant goal. For example, in 2002, the last time U.S. and Canadian toxic release inventories were compiled for the Great Lakes basin, over 4,000 facilities reported releases or transfers of over 1.3 billion pounds of pollutants. Discharges directly to water actually *increased* from the last binational reckoning four years earlier.[7] And this only accounts for the 650 substances that require reporting. According to the two governments' *State of the Great Lakes 2007* report,

Some 70,000 commercial and industrial compounds are now in use, and an estimated 1,000 new chemicals are introduced each year. Several chemical categories have been identified as chemicals of emerging concern, including polybrominated diphenyl ethers (flame retardants), perfluorooctanyl sulfonate (PFOs) and carboxylates, chlorinated paraffins and naphthalenes, various pharmaceutical and personal care products, phenolics, and approximately 20 currently used pesticides. PBDEs, siloxanes and musks are now widespread in the Great Lakes environment. Implementation of a more systematic program for monitoring new persistent toxic substances in the Great Lakes will require significant investments in instrumentation and researchers.[8]

A second reason why we continue to find high levels of toxic substances in Great Lakes fish is the long retention capacity of the lakes, and the fact that these substances remain in the sediments of our rivers and harbors and in thousands of leaking landfills along their shores. They are a legacy common to all the Areas of Concern, including six in New York State—the Buffalo River, Niagara River, Eighteenmile Creek (Niagara County), Rochester Embayment, Oswego River, and the St. Lawrence River at Massena—none of which has been cleaned up to the point where the fish advisories could be removed. (Although the Oswego River was officially delisted in 2006, the AOC fish advisories remain. See chapter 9).

On the basis of such indicators, the lower end of the Great Lakes ecosystem appears to be in the most trouble. The *State of the Great Lakes 2007* report rated the health of Lakes Erie and Ontario as "mixed" to "poor" in terms of most of the contaminants measured in fish and waterfowl. These revealed higher levels of PCBs, DDT, and mirex in Lake Ontario than anywhere else in the Great Lakes. No real surprise, as the two lower Great Lakes are the smallest and therefore the most vulnerable to pollution, and are at the receiving end of highly industrialized rivers—the Detroit and the Niagara. Twenty-one Areas of Concern are located in the watersheds of these two lakes and their connecting channels.

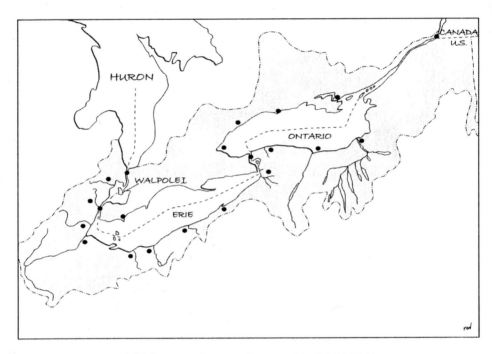

1.2. LOWER LAKES AREAS OF CONCERN

A WATER ETHIC

IN 1998, while working for a binational Great Lakes environmental
coalition, Great Lakes United, I attended a series of ten public hearings
across the Great Lakes–St. Lawrence River basin to gather citizens' testimony on water quality and to present those findings to the region's representatives in Washington, D.C., and Ottawa. Listening to people talk
about what was happening to the water, fish, wildlife, and human health
in their communities was a deeply moving experience, especially in
Detroit, where the longest, angriest, and most enlightening of all the
hearings took place. The highlight was a speaker from Walpole Island
First Nation, an indigenous community in Lake St. Clair, sometimes
called the "sixth Great Lake," located midway between Lakes Huron and
Erie. Walpole Island is just upstream from Detroit and the Detroit River,
and downstream from "Chemical Valley," and Sarnia, the "chemical capital of Canada," where more than 40 percent of Canadian bulk chemicals

are manufactured. Chemical spills to the river routinely threaten water quality in Lake St. Clair, causing the Walpole Island First Nation to shut down its drinking water intakes, assuming it is notified in time.

Other affected downstream communities have invested in an alternative supply, and now pipe their water down from Lake Huron. But the Walpole Island First Nation elected not to do this because, as the speaker said, "It would not have served the wildlife and the people who still consume the wildlife. It would have looked like we're giving up on the river, like we were saying, 'Okay, Chemical Valley, you can have the river between Sarnia and Imperial Chemical Industries.'"[9]

Walpole Island acted on the basis of an ethic that makes our usual ways of dealing with environmental pollution—say, leveraging a fine for a permit violation—look halfhearted at best. This was a decision more in keeping with the land ethic advocated by Wisconsin conservationist Aldo Leopold: "Examine each question in terms of what is ethically and esthetically right, as well as what is economically expedient. A thing is right when it tends to preserve the integrity, stability and beauty of the biotic community. It is wrong when it tends otherwise."[10]

There are many reasons why this is not an easy ethic to live by, not the least of which is the fact that stable biotic communities are increasingly hard to find. Most of us relative newcomers to the Great Lakes region have little idea of what its native communities looked like or how they functioned before they were "improved," harvested, or otherwise appropriated. So before we can even begin to act on a Leopoldian ethic, we need to ask questions. How did this river (lake, aquifer) work before it became a drain (industrial sewer, canal, power reservoir)? What life did it support? How did precolonial residents live here and what can we learn from their knowledge and stories of the region?

My interest in such questions is not to set impossible goals for restoring some imagined "pristine" wilderness condition, but to better understand the ecosystems that coevolved here over the millennia so that we can work with rather than against them. Perhaps the most important "take-home message" from these river explorations is that the seeds and remnants of indigenous ecologies are still here, waiting to be recognized and properly valued.

PART I

THE NIAGARA FRONTIER

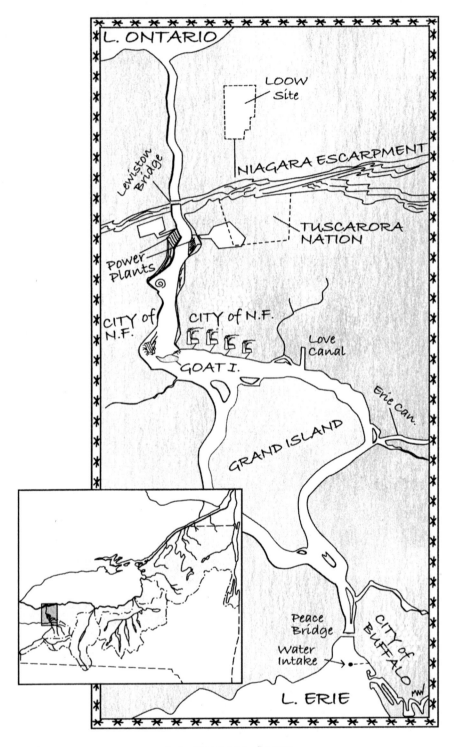

2.1. NIAGARA RIVER

TWO

WHAT IS NIAGARA?

It was not taken by surprise, but seemed to have anticipated,
in all its course through the broad lakes, that it must pour
their collected waters down this height.
                                    —Nathaniel Hawthorne

MY MOST FREQUENT EXPERIENCE of the Niagara River is crossing
over it on the Peace Bridge into Canada, usually in a procession of
NAFTA[1] trucks. There's plenty of time to enjoy the view, which is
especially good at about 3 P.M. on winter solstice when the ice on
Lake Erie is beginning to sheet up behind the ice boom to the west,
backlit by the lowering sun. The bridge crosses just where the lake
constricts into the first set of rapids on the river, a place where the
color and texture of the water changes, as landscape architect Frederick Law Olmsted once noted—where the funneling Great Lakes have
cut an "Emerald Channel" deep into the lake-riverbed. That quaint
little round brick building out there, directly over the Emerald Channel, is Buffalo's water intake, wisely placed upstream from the city's
sewage outfalls in 1913, after cholera and typhoid epidemics had culled
the city's populace a few times.

Sometimes I cross back on the Lewiston Bridge, 20 miles downstream, to see the river just released from the factory where it has been
turning turbines all day, all night for decades, looking spent and insignificant between two massive hydroelectric plants, giant cash registers

carved into opposing gorge walls. Sometimes I bring out-of-town guests to the place between these two bridges (where the Niagara River makes its spectacular fall) to spend an exhausting day parking the car and navigating through the tawdry blare of tourist distractions.

My *tai chi* teacher, a Chinese healer who survived the Great Leap Forward and the Cultural Revolution, came to Buffalo because of its nearness to Niagara Falls. A large photo of the falls dominates her living room, next to scrolls depicting the moving harmony between yang and yin, energy and receptivity, sun and earth. I have attended with her a huge Buddhist temple on the Canadian side of the river gorge, just downstream from the falls—the World Peace Temple of Ten Thousand Buddhas—located there apparently for the same reason she is here, because of the *chi,* the life force, of Niagara.

To Curly of the Three Stooges, "Niagara Falls" meant a beating from Moe who was mesmerized into violence every time Curly spoke those two words. "What words?" and so went the famous "Slowly I turned" routine for the honeymooning stooges in *Gents without Cents* (1944). Niagara's principal cities, Buffalo and the two cities of Niagara Falls, seem to have been hypnotized by the river's power in much the same half-witted way. In trying to capture it, to build economies on the basis of it, we have approached it like thugs, like stooges, resulting, at best, in a tacky glamour; at worst, in wanton destruction, though always with the best of intentions. And so it goes.

> Someone asks, "What more can Niagara do for us?"
> Someone answers, "Niagara Falls."
> And slowly we turn
> step-by-step,
> inch by inch,
> we trash it again.

I propose we ask another question: What is Niagara? Besides horsepower and scenery, what is it that we have here exactly? What is the river's natural history? How has it functioned in the region's cultural geography? In short, before we add any more decorations, siphon off any more water, or blow any more holes into the gorge, is there anything here we should know about?

TWO KEY ELEMENTS IN
GREAT LAKES GEOMORPHOLOGY

THE FIRST ELEMENT is captured in the name. *Nyah'-ga-rah* is a French version of the Mohawk pronunciation of the Neutral Nation's name for the river, *On-gui-aaha-a,* meaning "neck," says Orasmus Marshall, an early historian of this region.[2] Only 35 miles long, the Niagara River is less a river than a connecting channel, taking the long step down from the perch of the four inland Great Lakes, at roughly 600 feet above sea level, to the lowlands of Lake Ontario, the St. Lawrence River, and the Atlantic Ocean. Most of the drop, over 300 feet, is accomplished at the river's rapids and falls. The best place to experience the vastness, the "unlimitedness" of the Great Lakes water supply, is standing at the brink of Niagara Falls.

Got water?
Oh yeah.

In his 1834 sketch, "My Visit to Niagara," Nathaniel Hawthorne wrote one of the great descriptions of this outpour:

I was conscious of nothing but the great river, rolling calmly into the abyss, rather descending than precipitating itself, and acquiring tenfold majesty from its unhurried motion. It came like the march of Destiny. It was not taken by surprise, but seemed to have anticipated, in all its course through the broad lakes, that it must pour their collected waters down this height.

This height of land is the second key element. It is part of a landform that is far older than the Great Lakes and much larger than the cliff of exposed bedrock we see at Niagara Falls. It is a 1,000-mile-long serpentine ridge, a major defining element in the Great Lakes basin from central New York to Illinois. From Niagara Falls, it extends west and north through Ontario to the tip of the Bruce Peninsula, where it submerges briefly into Lake Huron and emerges again as Manitoulin Island before arcing south through Michigan's Upper Peninsula and down through Wisconsin's Door County, slicing off Green Bay from Lake Michigan.

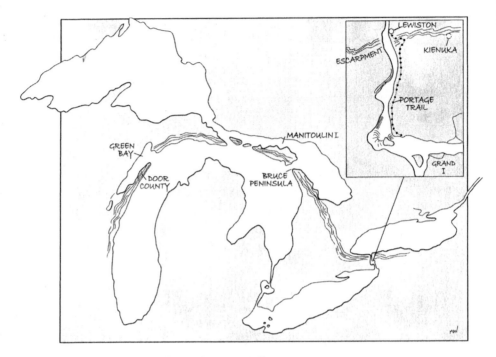

2.2. NIAGARA ESCARPMENT

I have heard many theories about what made the Niagara Escarpment. A tribal member of the Chippewas of Nawash, who live on one
of its most dramatic sections on the Bruce Peninsula, told me it is an
ancient coral reef, and, from the amount of fossil coral found in any
square foot of the blue bedrock exposed there, coral reefs are surely part
of the story. A common theory in western New York is that it marks a
fault line through the region, and though there is little evidence of that,
old tectonics are likely somehow involved. Whatever caused its particular meanders through the basin, its physical composition is consistent
throughout: layers of sedimentary rock dating back over 350 million
years, and angled up to 3 degrees from horizontal, make up a cliff
capped by hard, erosion-resistant limestone or dolomite. Wind, water,
and ice erosion have pretty much cleaned the slate in the Great Lakes
basin of the intervening 350 million years' worth of prehistoric record.
About all that remains under the frosting of glacial debris is the Paleo-
zoic serving plate with this hard edge running through it, a rocky spine

that sometimes accommodated trails and roads through the otherwise unbroken expanse of Great Lakes forest.

FROM WAR TRAIL TO PEACE TRAIL

ONE OF THE FIRST PEOPLE we know of by name in connection with the Niagara Escarpment is Jikonsahseh, or "the Peace Queen." She is thought to have been of the Neutral Nation, a people who lived on the Niagara Peninsula north of Lake Erie to just east of the Niagara River. The French called them Neutral or "Neuter" because of the place they occupied geographically, economically, politically—between the Haudenosaunee (Iroquois) to the east and the Wendat (Huron) to the west and north. That the Neutral people were at peace with both sides when the French first encountered them in the early 1600s may be credited in part to the tradition and teachings of the first Peace Queen who lived here at least a century earlier.

The Niagara Frontier was not always so peaceful. Seneca scholar John Mohawk describes how it was before the founding of the Haudenosaunee Confederacy. "This was a time of great sorrow and terror for the Haudenosaunee. All order and safety had broken down completely and the rule of the headhunter dominated the culture . . . [each] killing sparked a spiral of vengeance and reprisal which found assassins stalking the Northeastern woodlands in a never ending senseless bloodletting."[3]

Jikonsahseh's name is associated with a place—"Kienuka" or "fort"—dug into the Niagara Escarpment's north face adjacent to the present-day Tuscarora territory. Although well known to archaeologists and the Tuscaroras, the site is not marked or publicly accessible, nor is it really visible unless you know what you're looking for. The cliff commands a wide view of the main Haudenosaunee east–west trail, sometimes called the War Trail (now Route 104). Centuries of erosion have carved deep cracks and passageways through its bedrock, places that could conceal many people.

Jikonsahseh, according to most stories, was first a warmonger; she profited at the location by trading information to enemies on both sides. Yet she became the first convert to the Great Law of Peace. "The Peacemaker sought out the most remarkable survivors of this random and undeclared war and he initiated discussions with them," says Mohawk.

"[H]e offered the idea that all human beings possess the power of rational thought and that in the belief in rational thought is to be found the power to create peace." Oneida singer and storyteller Joanne Shenandoah continues this story: "[He said] he was to form a world union of nations, all bound by a set of rules he called the Great Law of Peace. This divine message of goodness was to take root in the hearts of the most terrible peoples of all, the warring tribes of the Iroquois territories . . . He had come to the territory of the Neutral Nation because he had heard of Jikonsahseh and wanted to persuade her to support his great plan."[4]

According to some versions of the story, it is Jikonsahseh who persuades the Seneca Nation to join the confederacy. Because of Jikonsahseh's early allegiance to the Great Law, "the Peacemaker would give women the power to select and depose the leaders of their nations. They would be given the title of 'clanmother.' The people would choose clanmothers to direct the families while having the responsibility as lifegivers of deciding upon all matters relating to life." In traditional Haudenosaunee communities like the Tuscarora, clan mothers still bear these responsibilities.

"Jikonsahseh" or "Peace Queen" became a title and office in the confederacy handed down through the centuries. The last Peace Queen was Caroline Mount Pleasant, who died in 1892 and whose family home now lies at the bottom of the Niagara power reservoir.

The Great Law of Peace is embodied in the articles of the Haudenosaunee Confederacy, a code of principles and practices for democratic self-governance and for resolving conflicts within and outside the Six Nations. Contemporary historians have shown how Benjamin Franklin and others modeled key provisions for representative democracy in the U.S. Constitution on the Great Law of the Confederacy, but they tend to overlook the contribution of Jikonsahseh and the social structures for peace invented on the Niagara Frontier.[5]

GETTING OVER THE ESCARPMENT

BY THE TIME Nathaniel Hawthorne saw them, Niagara's falls were already well on their way to becoming a pay-per-view tourist spectacle, with private landowners charging visitors a fee to view the mighty cataracts through a peephole in their fences. Hawthorne's consciousness of "nothing but the great river" was a frame of mind attained only by screening out the surrounding clutter, a process that led him to bemoan, as have many who've come after, "Oh, that I had never heard of Niagara til I beheld it! Blessed were the wanderers of old, who heard its deep roar sounding through the woods, as the summons to an unknown wonder, and approached its awful brink."

Father Louis Hennepin, chaplain to Robert de LaSalle and a crew of thirty-two men searching for "the Great River passage to Mexico," left the earliest record we have of a European's impression of Niagara Falls, based on their arrival there in 1678.

> Betwixt the Lake Ontario and Erie, there is a vast and prodigious Cadence of Water which falls down after a surprizing and astonishing manner insomuch that the Universe does not afford its Parallel . . . The Waters which fall from this horrible Precipice do foam and boyl after the most hideous manner imaginable, making an outrageous Noise, more terrible than that of Thunder; for when the Wind blows out of the South, their dismal roaring may be heard more than Fifteen Leagues off.[6]

Yet even Hennepin's virgin view was framed by an agenda. Everything depended on New France getting over "the Three Mountains," as Hennepin called the terraced escarpment, to find the water route to the continental interior with its proverbial wealth of furs, gold, and unsaved souls. And finally New France did climb up, hauling anchors, cannons, and tackle for the 60-ton *Griffin* over the "horrible Precipice." "Our Anchors were so big, that four Men had much ado to carry one." (In 2006, performance artist Elinor Whidden and her crew reenacted this feat, carrying a disassembled Ford Taurus step-by-step up the old Portage Trail, as a comment on our "apathetic acceptance of the daily commute.")

The *Griffin* itself and its cargo of 12,000 furs disappeared forever on the return trip from Green Bay, just months after it first set sail. Eventually, however, the trail up the escarpment at Lewiston became the most fought over strategic point on the river. A 1750 Annual Register of the fur trade reports "over two hundred Senecas were employed in carrying furs over the portage, at the rate of twenty pence a pack for the entire distance." The Seneca are said to have called the Lewiston portage *Dug-jih-heh-oh,* meaning "walking on all fours."

From an ecosystem perspective, the escarpment served as a natural protective barrier for the upper Great Lakes for several thousand years. Nonnative invasive species like the sea lamprey had no easy access to these inland seas until we built bypasses like the Erie and Welland canals.

LOVE AND THE MESMERIZING VISION
OF UNLIMITED CHEAP POWER

WITH THE INVENTION of the electric generator, the seemingly endless abundance of falling water at Niagara gained new meaning. Between 1880 and 1907, Niagara's average flow was calculated at 212,000 cubic feet per second, sufficient to power the whole of North America at the time. Technology and infrastructure for capturing all that energy quickly grew to the point that, were it not for the limits placed by the Boundary Waters Treaty in 1909, we could take it all. But the U.S.–Canada treaty requires that 100,000 cubic feet per second must flow over Niagara Falls during daylight hours in tourist season, and a minimum of 50,000 cubic feet per second at all other times. In short, for most of the year over 75 percent of Niagara's flow is diverted through tunnels into New York's and Ontario's power reservoirs and the falls themselves are a bypass, allotted just enough water to cover the crest.

Early schemes for harnessing Niagara "for the benefit of mankind" were as utopian in promise as they were monumental in scope, a rhetorical pairing that continues to front the development of major river diversions across the world—from Nehru's "Dams are the temples of modern India" policy, to China's equation of nation-building with the Three Gorges Dam, its largest construction project since the Great Wall. Perhaps only the most inflated prose can justify the costs, including the social and environmental costs of these mega-hydroprojects, and override the basic questions that industrializing parts of the world are beginning to ask themselves as these costs become more apparent. Who owns the river? Who owns the fish? Who will profit? What will be lost?

In the early 1890s, William T. Love turned up in Niagara County and began buying land and issuing press releases about the "extraordinary conditions" for Model City "now building, destined to be the Greatest Manufacturing City in America." Key to it all was "unlimited cheap power." Love planned to divert water from the upper river by way of an 8-mile-long canal leading to his own powerhouse at the base of the Niagara Escarpment. At the time, there were few or no restrictions on water diversions, private or public. The country was suffering an economic depression. Model City gained enthusiastic, uncritical support from the region's newspapers. In fact, what we know of Love's venture is largely based on the almost daily coverage of his actions, hopes, and dreams provided by *The Daily Cataract*, the *Niagara Falls Journal,* and the *Niagara Falls Gazette.*

Love promised to attract industries from across the nation by offering free factory sites, free power for forty years, and a resident workforce of 100,000 workers. He had none of these things, but believed they would materialize from the "extraordinary conditions" at Niagara Falls. Model City would be a metropolis of wide boulevards and public squares, devoid of tenements and liquor; every man would own his own home. New York's Governor Flowers was sold. "If that charter for a model city is handled properly, eventually there will be a city of 2,000,000 inhabitants at Lewiston," he predicted (*Niagara Falls Gazette*, May 17, 1893). Niagara County's entire population at the time was under 75,000. Flowers granted Love powers to condemn and take over property. By 1893, Love had acquired rights to 20,000 acres of prime fruit and dairy land on the Lake Ontario plain, and he controlled the Niagara Power and Development Company. He cleared and graded orchards, forests, and farms, put up a few buildings, and dug about a mile of his canal.

Then his financial supporters deserted him.

In January 1906, the front page of the *Gazette* announced Love's comeback with an "Aragain Army," a Niagara in reverse, to be financed by offering building lots for just one dollar down and a dollar per month for the first 5,000 comers, on condition that a workforce of 100,000 would finally enlist. But by then the extraordinary conditions at Niagara Falls had begun to evaporate. First, the invention and installation of alternating current made it possible to transmit electricity over long distances, eliminating the location advantage of Model City. Then, in response to public outcry that water power diversions were destroying the beauty of Niagara Falls, Congress passed the Burton Act (1906), limiting the amount of water that could be diverted on the American side to what already was being taken. In 1909, the Boundary Waters Treaty superceded the Burton Act and placed limits on total water diversion from Niagara and from all U.S.–Canada boundary waters.

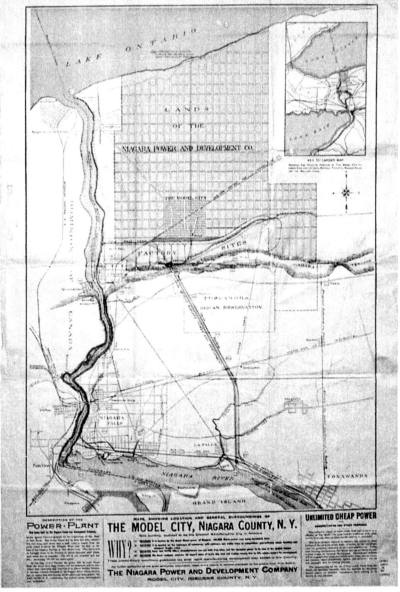

2.3. LOVE'S VISION FOR MODEL CITY. COURTESY OF
THE NIAGARA FALLS. N.Y.. PUBLIC LIBRARY. LOCAL
HISTORY DEPARTMENT.

Love's bankrupt corporation was sold at auction in 1910.

"It is not clear where William T. Love came from or, for that matter, where he went," said *The Buffalo News* in 1993, the one hundredth anniversary of the inception of Model City. However, he did leave a lasting impression on the Niagara Frontier. The heart of Model City became, literally, a wasteland. In the early 1940s, the federal government acquired 7,500 acres—the Lower Ontario Ordinance Works or LOOW—to manufacture dynamite and then to serve as a repository for radioactive material, beginning with atomic bomb wastes from the Manhattan Project. Chemical Waste Management, the only licensed, commercial, hazardous waste landfill in the Northeast, occupies about 700 acres of the LOOW. It is the final destination for hundreds of thousands of tons of toxic wastes from thirty states, several Canadian provinces, and Puerto Rico, and is the second largest PCB landfill in the country. Modern Landfill, a vast municipal garbage dump also located there, shares its administrative building with the old Model City post office serving a small handful of residents. Public schools for the Towns of Lewiston and Porter are there too, within the original LOOW footprint, just a few miles away from Lake Ontario and the Niagara River.

Love's canal fragment in the City of Niagara Falls gradually filled with garbage, fly ash from waste incinerators, and about 20,000 tons of chemical wastes from Hooker Chemical and its predecessors. In the early 1950s, houses were built along the canal (now filled, capped, invisible) and, in 1953, the Niagara Falls Board of Education decided it would be a good site for the school needed to serve this growing community, so they purchased it from Hooker and built the 96th Street School there.

Over the next two decades, chemicals leaked into the playing fields from time to time and there was growing evidence of chronic illness in the Love Canal neighborhood. But it was not until the spring of 1977, following a record-breaking winter of 199 inches of snow, that the toxic brew seriously overflowed into neighboring creeks, basements, and yards, including the 96th Street schoolyard. On August 2, 1978, state health commissioner Robert P. Whalen made Love Canal world news when he warned of "a great and imminent peril to the health of the general public residing at or near the said site as a result of exposure to toxic substances emanating from such site." Eventually about nine hundred people, many of them ill, were relocated, and Love's canal took on global meaning as a sort of *Amityville Horror* of buried chemical pollution come back to haunt us.

MOSES AND THE MESMERIZING VISION OF UNLIMITED CHEAP POWER

FIFTY YEARS AFTER William Love abandoned his canal, Robert Moses, head of the New York State Power Authority, was able to part the waters and move earth on a scale Love had only dreamed of. Moses' grand vision was to industrialize the Great Lakes region by providing cheap power for manufacturing and by opening (blasting, dredging, widening, deepening) the shipping channels for international trade. In partnership with Ontario Hydro, the New York Power Authority first constructed the Moses-Saunders Dam on the St. Lawrence River in 1959 as part of the St. Lawrence Seaway Project. The Niagara Power Project, one of the largest hydropower plants in the country, was completed two years later.

In 2007, the Federal Energy Regulatory Commission renewed the Niagara Project's operating license for another fifty years. As a condition of renewal, the commission required the New York Power Authority to compensate host communities for "the effects of operation." Although this phrase seriously limited the scope for addressing damages, the process leading up to relicensing unleashed an intense discussion among river communities about the social and environmental costs of the Niagara Power Project.

Part of that discussion centered on indirect (and therefore non-compensated) impacts. Cheap power and plentiful water drew to Niagara one of the largest concentrations of chemical industries in the world. Some say the legacy of hazardous waste dumps they left behind turned the region into a "sacrifice zone"—a chemical dump for the nation. Chemical waste landfills have been the major sources of contaminants to fish and wildlife in the Niagara River, Lake Ontario, and the St. Lawrence River. Love Canal was but one of many buried channels and tunnels dug into the fractured bedrock surrounding Niagara Falls that conducted long-forgotten toxic wastes to the river.

Nor did the commission consider damages caused by the project's construction, which occurred before the environmental impact statement process required by the 1970 National Environmental Protection Act. Nevertheless, during the relicensing review, the public began to grasp the magnitude of the project's footprint on the region. Physically it took over 4,000 acres of river and near-river land, including the blasting and transport of millions of cubic yards of rock and earth from the riverbed and gorge that were dumped on other parts of the riverbed, gorge, and escarpment. Land for the facility also came off the tax roles since the New York Power Authority is exempt from paying property taxes.

The power reservoir and a segment of the high-voltage transmission line corridor took 550 acres of Tuscarora land. For Haudenosaunee communities across the state this was an episode in a larger displacement, a "second trail of tears," beginning with the 1959 St. Lawrence Seaway and Moses-Saunders Dam, which replaced traditional Mohawk uses of that river with an industrial complex much like the one on Niagara. The Niagara project was completed in 1961, followed by the Kinzua Dam on the Allegheny River in 1966, which flooded 9,000 acres of Seneca land. The Mohawk, Seneca, and Tuscarora nations fought intense, expensive legal battles in all three cases, claiming violations of sovereignty and treaty rights—and lost.[7] The Tuscaroras did succeed in limiting the project's presence on their land from the originally proposed 1,380 acres to less than half that.

Prior to relicensing, the New York Power Authority commissioned dozens of studies to assess the impacts of operation. Not surprisingly, most of these studies concluded that the impacts were insignificant, except possibly the effects on aquatic life of daily water level changes of 1 to 12 feet per day, depending on where you were in the river.[8] But changes in operation were also off the negotiating table, so, in the end, host communities came away with cash settlements totaling $391 million, adjusted for inflation, to be paid out over the next fifty years. They also received an allotment of low-cost power, but not enough to offset the fact that the Niagara region pays some of the highest electricity rates in the country.

"The one unqualified success that came out of the deal for the community is a set-aside of $145.6 million to build a greenway along the length of the Niagara River," said The Buffalo News in an investiga-

2.4. TUSCARORA PROTEST. *COURIER EXPRESS.* 1958.
COURTESY OF BUFFALO STATE COLLEGE ARCHIVES AND
BUFFALO AND ERIE COUNTY HISTORICAL SOCIETY.

tive report entitled "Power Failure" (May 1, 2007). Buffalo Niagara
Riverkeeper and many other environmental and community groups
played an important role in developing an ecologically based Niagara
River Greenway Plan and in mobilizing its unanimous approval by
thirteen river municipalities. Greenway funds, along with another $60
million "ecological fund" for habitat improvements on the river, now
represent the best chance to mitigate some of the damages caused by
the power project.

You might argue that a license to operate for fifty more years
should have required the Power Authority, say, to reduce the project's
operational impacts on the river ecosystem, to lower the Niagara
region's electricity rates, and to invest some percentage of its profits in
developing energy efficiencies and green alternatives, especially given
probable lower river flows due to climate change. But federal energy
policy sets the ground rules for what is negotiable and by these rules
none of these issues was ever on the table. Federal and state energy
policies categorize even this mega-hydropower installation as "green"

2.5. "FALLS FOLLIES." MAY 20. 1962. COURTESY OF
THE *NIAGARA GAZETTE*.

and do not admit challenges to certain blanket assumptions: that it is
good for the economy, good for the environment, and good for us, the
ever hungrier consumers of power.

CLOSING THE CIRCLE: FREEING NIAGARA

IT IS HARD TO BELIEVE that ten years *before* William Love obtained the
state's unstinting support for Model City, and two generations before
Robert Moses, American and Canadian preservationists fought and
won a sixteen-year-long landmark battle to protect and restore the natural beauty of Niagara Falls. Here we must backtrack a bit to recall that,
by the mid–1800s, factories, mills, and fences (with peepholes) lined the
river and surrounded the falls. The magnitude of the visual blight
inspired landscape architect Frederick Law Olmsted, architect Henry

Hobson Richardson, and others to organize a binational campaign to "free Niagara." Lord Dufferin, the governor general of Canada, was supportive. He publicly criticized "the various squatting interests that have taken possession of every point of vantage at the Falls." Various governors of New York over the next two decades alternatively gave or withdrew their support. Finally, in 1883, Governor Grover Cleveland signed a bill authorizing appropriation of lands at Niagara Falls for a state park. In 1885, the bill passed, creating the 112-acre Niagara Reservation "for the purpose of preserving the scenery of the Falls of Niagara, and of restoring said scenery to its natural condition." In 1887, the Province of Ontario established the 154-acre Queen Victoria Niagara Falls Park, dedicated to the same purpose.

Much has been written about the significance of the Free Niagara Movement and the precedent-setting legislation that established these parks. For the first time in the histories of both countries, the preservation of the aesthetics of the natural environment was made a legitimate public endeavor.[9] As a property rights issue, the Free Niagara Movement positioned those who believed that Niagara Falls was a unique natural area that should be accessible to all, against private property interests who thought that the Niagara experience, including the right to look at the falls, should be purchased.

In New York, the costs of appropriation worked out to twenty-eight cents per person, which the taxpayers supported overwhelmingly.[10] The state tore down 150 buildings and hired the landscape architecture firm of Olmsted and Vaux to develop and implement a plan that would return the land to a natural setting. Their plan called for the removal of mills, factories, and "other industrial accommodations," removal of "illumination apparatus," and removal of the gorge railway. It prohibited exhibitions involving displays in and over the water and promoted removal of roads and paved walkways in favor of pathways. It allowed only pedestrian access to Goat Island, where botanist Asa Gray found the greatest variety of plants of any place in North America due to the unique river and mist microclimate; and it eliminated all buildings, including restaurants and other tourist accommodations, from the reservation.

Today, elements of the Olmsted–Vaux plan are still visible but losing ground beneath the Moses overlay and a steady accumulation of pavement, snack shops, souvenir booths, and illumination apparatus—

basically all the things the Free Niagara Movement set out to eliminate 120 years ago. As head of both the New York Power Authority *and* the office of state parks, Robert Moses was almost able to cover Olmsted's vision with his own, which centered on the power plant and "power vistas" along the Robert Moses Parkway dominating the gorge rim. He built a 282-foot-tall steel and glass observation tower overhanging the gorge at the American falls, a structure that has come to symbolize the tourism blight on the Niagara Falls landscape.

And so it goes. Slowly we turn, and, step-by-step, a second Free Niagara Movement is forming. Some river advocates, like the Niagara Heritage Partnership, want to see the Olmsted–Vaux plan fully implemented, which would include tearing down part of the Robert Moses Parkway and other structures encroaching on the falls and gorge. They regard a clear boundary as a good strategy both for protecting the natural beauty of the park and for directing tourism-based economic development to the impoverished city of Niagara Falls, New York.

Others propose seeking a UN designation for the Niagara River corridor as a "World Biosphere Reserve," following the model of the Niagara Escarpment in Ontario, which gained this status in 1990. In the case of the escarpment, what was once a rocky trail through an unbroken expanse of forest has become the last significant wooded corridor in southern Ontario. Strict regulations now guide development on and around the escarpment, and a land trust is working to purchase and protect critical habitats along its spine.

Proponents of an "International Niagara Peace Park" see the Niagara region as ripe for a status, conferred by the World Conservation Union, that would acknowledge and build on all the natural and cultural resources associated with the transboundary river—including the unique biodiversity of the escarpment and gorge and an almost two hundred-year tradition of peace between the United States and Canada. "The goal is nothing less than to create a model for collaborative action behind an integrated strategy for sustainable development that can transform our region and instruct the world."[11]

All these efforts have one thing in common. They seek to recover what is Niagara: the river in all its particularity as landform and habitat, as Great Lakes outlet and barrier, and as a political boundary and neutral zone where nations that were hopelessly at war have managed— more than once—to innovate a long-lived peace.

INTERLUDE

Harmonic Convergence, Niagara Falls

AUGUST 17, 1987. We leave at 5 A.M., in league with all the others who are convening even now at their chosen spots on the planet. Our destination: Terrapin Point, the cusp of Goat Island dividing the American from the Canadian falls.

I have a letter from Seneca Wolf Clan elder Twylah Nitsch, encouraging me to bring along friends and a jar of water from home. She sends information that the Hopi, Mayan, and Aztec calendars all predict today as marking the beginning of the last quarter-century in a 5,200-year cycle—the beginning of the end of the battle-worn Fourth World and the transition to the Fifth, which opens in the year 2012. The celestial sign is a double triangle Star of David, denoting Earth's coming into alignment with the hub of the galaxy, a configuration that won't occur again for another five millennia.

A clear shot straight to the center of the Milky Way may be just what we need, I tell my seven-year-old son and the two little soccer buddies who come with us. Today we play on a field that includes some of the coolest places on Earth: Macchu Pichu, Stonehenge, Mount Olympus, Mount Fuji, Mount Shasta, the Ganges River, Niagara Falls. This is big, kids. They listen groggily in the backseat, glad to be missing practice this morning.

Out on Goat Island we watch the sun rise over the Nabisco grain elevator, and then a cloud, shaped like a Thunderbird, appears below the sun. A rainbow forms behind us, across the gorge, and hangs there for an hour or so. Everyone stands in their own thoughts, facing east, encompassed in the roar of Niagara.

As the day comes on, the crowd takes over—people of all colors, in saris, dashikis, tie-dyed T-shirts, black leather and spikes, dreadlocks, mohawks, hair dyed every stripe of the rainbow. Someone has organized a water ceremony. People come forward with little jars of water, pronounce the name of its source, and pour it into a basin. We say "Scajaquada," remembering the little falls in the cemetery where we collected the day before. One of the native men from the drumming circle gives thanks to the waters of the world for quenching our thirst and providing us with strength. "With one mind, we send greetings and thanks to the spirit of water." He pours the contents of the basin into the river.

Other than that, people pretty much do their own thing. The Sufis twirl, the Native Americans drum and sing, the hippies burn incense and sage, total strangers hug, spontaneous circles of dancing and chanting erupt here and there.

A spin-off from the Outer Circle Orchestra, the 12/8 Path, leads a Conga line weaving through the crowd. The tail end pulls us in. We're glad to be incorporated, wiggling our collective butts to the rhythm. *Boom boom Bop bop Hip! Hip!*

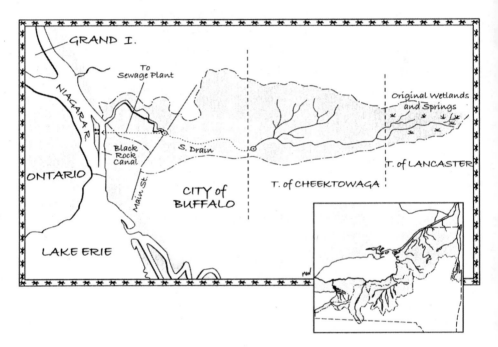

3.1. Scajaquada Creek Watershed

THREE

SCAJAQUADA

Portrait of an Urban Creek

It was ruled that the creek must go.
—Margaret Fess, *Buffalo Courier Express*

BUFFALO'S SCAJAQUADA (Sca-ják-wa-da) Creek is only 15 miles long, much of it underground, meandering vertically between an upper world of sunlight and air and a netherworld of springs and sewer drains. It is a veritable Frankenstein's monster of engineering experiments designed to protect us from it—most of them failed. Why, you may well ask, is this insignificant *drain* included on the roster with New York's big-hitting Great Lakes rivers?

I turn to Scajaquada as a case study in the last century's approach to urban planning. Once at the heart of Buffalo's water supply and Olmsted park design, the creek succumbed, bit by bit, to procedures designed to put it out of the way. Because I live near Scajaquada Creek, about 3 miles inland from its mouth on the Niagara River, I have had ample opportunity to study the results of these decisions, especially since the city reversed its disappearing policy and built a public trail along the last segment. Now, for the first time in generations, the creek is accessible in the Parkside and Black Rock neighborhoods through which it flows.

A few of us began walking this path and noticing its wonders—a pair of resident beavers, a population of enormous snapping turtles, black-crowned night-herons hunting from the trash racks. Eventually, we became the "Parkside Greens" and unofficially adopted the waterway that spawned us. Curious about the whole creek, we traced as much of it as we could on foot and searched the public records for clues to its earlier existence. Here is what we found.

AT ITS MOUTH ON THE NIAGARA RIVER

THE INTERNATIONAL RAILROAD BRIDGE spins open on its axis and a big coal ship, the *Calcite II*, passes into the Black Rock lock. As the lock fills with water, the laker rises, its keel looming over us. We are in a nonplace, under the highway access ramps where Scajaquada enters the Niagara River. The ship is riding high; we infer it has delivered its coal to the Huntley electricity plant further downriver and is now heading back to Lake Erie, probably to the coal motherload outlet at Erie, Pennsylvania. This coordinated movement of giant infrastructure with no visible human operators is all the more impressive for being so "behind the scenes."

Moses Shongo, a Seneca healer and historian who lived a century ago, describes the strategic importance of this shoreline where creek, islands, and rock triangulated into a spirit refuge and Niagara River crossing place:

> The word *Ohs-dáe*, in onondaga's tongue means rock, of immense dimensions, and the word *dyus-dae-gah-a*, is made up of the first word, with a little change in first syllable and the last two syllables *gah-a*, making the meaning rock protruding out of the ground to river, according to Seneca traditions showing the place and name to be of a very ancient origin connected to the Spirit of thunder & lightning.
>
> Black Rock, *Dyus-dae-gah-a*, was the place and name that was known to ancient inhabitants or aborigines because it was 1 a place of refuge for the supposed Supernatural beings who frequented that spot . . . 2 an easy place to cross over on

account of the Island. all Iroquois crossed back and forth at this spot, the easiest place for landing.[1]

The black rock, a 300-foot-long, 5-foot-high formation of ebony-colored chert, was part of an underwater reef at the head of Niagara's upper rapids where Lake Erie narrows and concentrates. It was known for good fishing: 4-pound pickerel and lake trout; herring said to be so plentiful that three casts of a net would fill a barrel. Just downstream from the black rock, Squaw Island and Scajaquada Creek completed the configuration that made this bit of Great Lakes coastline so biologically rich and so significant over the centuries as a natural harbor.

Had you come along this shore in 1679, you might have witnessed a curious sight: not supernatural beings, but Frenchmen seeking not refuge, but furs—and hauling, half-sailing, a "moving Fortress" adorned with a flying griffin, an eagle, and five cannons, toward the mouth of Lake Erie. Father Hennepin recorded how LaSalle's men assembled the *Griffin* at the mouth of Cayuga Creek above Niagara Falls, how they sailed upriver to safe harbor in the strait between Squaw Island and Scajaquada, how they waited the summer for the right wind to carry them up into the lake. He also describes the Senecas' reaction: how they tried to set fire to the ship and kill the blacksmith in response to LaSalle's various betrayals; how they shouted *Gannorom*, "which in their Language signifies, That is wonderful" when the *Griffin* actually launched into Lake Erie.

> The Iroquese being return'd from Hunting Beavers, were mightily surpriz'd to see our Ship a-float, and called us *Otkon*, that is in their Language, Most penetrating Wits: For they could not apprehend how in so short a time we had been able to build so great a Ship, though it was but 60 Tuns. It might have been indeed call'd a moving Fortress; for all the Savages inhabiting the Banks of those Lakes and Rivers I have mention'd, for five hundred Leagues together, were fill'd with Fear as well as Admiration when they saw it. . . .
>
> The Wind veering to the North-East, and the Ship being well-provided, we made all Sail we could, and with the help of Twelve Men who hall'd from the Shoar, overcame the Rapidity of the Current and got up into the Lake. The Iroquese and

their Prisoners were much surpriz'd to see us in the Lake, and did not think before that, we should be able to overcome the Rapidity of the current: They cry'd several times *Gannorom*, to shew their Admiration.[2]

In 1818, you might have seen this whole scene strangely repeated when another history-making boat, the *Walk-in-the-Water*, the first steamboat to sail the lakes above the falls, was towed up to Lake Erie from the shipyards at the mouth of Scajaquada Creek.

In the first year of the War of 1812, the British and their Indian allies canoed across the Niagara River under cover of night to Black Rock landing, fought the local militia defending the harbor at Scajaquada Creek, and went on to burn down Buffalo, such as it was. Buffalo rebuilt and eventually prevailed over its rival village of Black Rock by dredging a harbor at the mouth of the Buffalo River, which would become the western terminus of the Erie Canal.

In 1824, the city fathers blasted out the black rock to make room for the Black Rock Canal section of the Erie Canal. The once strategic Squaw Island, located conveniently downstream from what would become the urban core, became Buffalo's dump and, in 1935, the site for its first sewage treatment plant.

ZONING FOR TURTLES

OLD MAPS of the last 2 miles of Scajaquada Creek show how this reach once naturally broadened to lake-size proportions as it approached the Niagara River. The grassy wetlands surrounding the Sca-

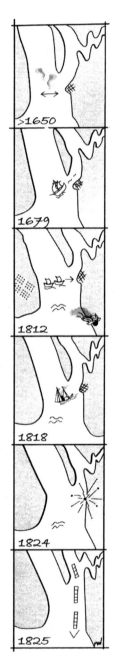

3.2. STORY OF BLACK ROCK

jaquada delta supported the great migrations of birds that used and still use the river corridor. A globally important bird area, Niagara today supports significant portions of the world's populations of Bonaparte's gull, herring gull, canvasback duck, and common merganser that stop over or winter here. One can only imagine how it was two hundred years ago. Straightening, narrowing, damming, and filling began in the early 1800s with Black Rock harbor and continued through the 1950s when the Scajaquada Expressway was built.

Throughout most of the twentieth century, Buffalo, like most Great Lakes cities, zoned its shoreline for manufacturing and used its rivers and nearshore waters for industrial processes and waste disposal. This excerpt from Buffalo's zoning code describes (rather than prescribes) the landscape of permitted "M2" uses whose legacy we live with today:

1. Boilermaking, structural steel or pipe works, drop hammers, locomotive or railway car manufacturing, railroad roundhouse shop, ship building and repair.
2. Brewing and distilling of beer.
3. Grain elevator, flour mill or cereal manufacture . . .
4. Junkyard, including auto wrecking or dismantling . . .
5. Manufacture and storage of acetylene gas, acid, ammonia, bleaching powder, chlorine, dextrine, disinfectant, enamel, fungicide, glucose, insecticide, lacquer, linoleum, paint, paper, pulp, perfume, potash, printing ink, shellac, starch, turpentine or varnish, or grinding colors by machine.
6. Manufacture, refining or distillation of asphalt, carbon, coal, coke, creosote, gas and tar.

Gas, steel, paint, and chemicals were all made on the lower creek, saturating soil and sediments with a familiar Great Lakes brew: benzene, toluene, xylene, lead, cyanide, polyaromatic hydrocarbons (PAHs), and polychlorinated biphenyls (PCBs). No one seemed to know or care that these pollutants would not be flushed away and disappear or that they would show up decades later in the food chain. For example, one recent study, designed to trace sources of PCBs and other contaminants to Lake Ontario, placed bluntnose minnows in cages at the mouths of sixteen streams tributary to the lake. Scajaquada Creek minnows showed by far the highest concentrations of PCBs, with mean values at 1,407 parts per billion—compared to a safety standard of no more than 100 parts per billion—posing "a severe threat to fish-eating consumers."[3]

Here in this abandoned industrial landscape, below the flow of the Scajaquada Expressway, we find the only dedicated public access to the creek, thanks to one person, Jesse Kregal, timpanist with the Buffalo Philharmonic Orchestra, runner, and principal visionary of the Scajaquada Pathway. Jogging through the silent corridor over twenty years ago, Jesse began imagining and then assembling the funds to build a 2-mile trail linking Buffalo's central city park to the Niagara Riverwalk. Dogged and diplomatic, he shepherded the project through to completion, enabling access to a stream, a history, and a quietly ongoing water life that even we who live nearby barely knew existed.

On May 1, 1993, after following the city's percussionist through the weird terrain of the sub-expressway M2 creek, we catalogued these uses that have yet to appear in the city's zoning code:

1. Foot-and-a-half-long snapping turtles sunning themselves on rocks
2. Great blue heron following the creek like a map upstream
3. Redwing blackbirds fanning, trilling
4. Long-stemmed grasses; beaver-cut trees
5. Grown men fishing all along
6. Black Rock kids playing junkyard baseball

THE SCAJAQUADA DRAIN

THE NEXT PIECE OF Scajaquada trickles from a pipe into the city's only cemetery, Forest Lawn, accompanied by waft of methane gas. It is a beautiful spot. From here, for about 100 yards, we find Scajaquada in its own natural shale and limestone ravine. Streamers of dried grass, paper, and plastic bags run through the lower branches of all the overhanging trees and shrubs at about 2 feet above ground, showing the high-water line established by the last big rain. Warblers sing from the tangled banks, jewel-headed mallards paddle through the pool below a two-step waterfall. I spend a morning here with a group of city high school teachers who are hoping to use the creek for biology field trips. Like miners panning for gold, we collect and sift through sediments and find nothing but a few bloodworms, a chrionomid fly larva associated with sewage sludge.

The flow itself seems miraculously to reappear, recovered from its 3½ mile stint under ground. A 1952 *Buffalo Courier Express* article recalls the Buffalo Sewer Authority's six-year (1922–1928) engineering project that sentenced this segment of the creek to life imprisonment in a drain:

> Thousands of Buffalonians cross a bridge on Main St. every day and don't know it. Other hundreds have a creek in their back-yards and don't know it. The subterranean creek is not a freak of nature, but a 4½ million dollar flood control and sanitation project . . .
>
> Buffalonians have not been denied a beauty spot. Hundreds of residents all along its route directed sewers into the water-way [and] used it to dump garbage, dead cats and refuse. During Spring freshets it often sent hunks of ice hurtling down Genesee St., flooded basements and washed out shrubbery. By Summer, when a stream would have been a welcome sight, it was nothing but a smelly trickle . . .
>
> After several years of study and debate, *it was ruled that the creek must go.* Construction of the huge underground passage was begun in the early '20s and the work of removing hun-dreds of tons of rock, trees, streets and bridges continued for five or six years. With only a few exceptions the underground waterway follows the original zigzag bed of the creek . . . The underground structure is 14 feet high, from 24 to 33 feet in width and is sunk underground from 15 to 30 feet.[4] (Italics mine)

The Lower Marine Historical Society has a photographic archive of the Scajaquada Drain construction, including a picture of a man holding up what appears to be a giant horseshoe crab found under Florida Street. "It was about three feet long, embedded in rock, and alive," said Cecil F. Seitz, the chief engineer. "We gave the thing to the Science Museum."[5] I checked, but museum accessions has no record of this gift. It remains one of the many mysteries of the creek's life underground.

Stranger still, given the apparent interest in sanitation, is how this project affected "Gala Water," the centerpiece of Buffalo's park system, a lake created when Frederick Law Olmsted dammed a portion of Scajaquada Creek in the 1880s. After the drain was completed, Gala Water evolved into a sewage lagoon, until the county health department finally proclaimed it a health hazard and closed public access. Let's take a closer look at what happened here, as it exemplifies the engineering of creeks into sewers in cities throughout the Great Lakes, and illustrates why this approach has failed to protect human and ecosystem health.

When it rains or the snow melts in built-up, paved-over urban and suburban areas, the water that can no longer be absorbed by soil flows into the nearest street drain. In the case of approximately 150 Great Lakes communities, including Buffalo, this is the same drain that collects and transports sewage. The more pavement, the less water infiltrates into the ground, the more runs off into sewers. In the lower Great Lakes region especially, where sprawling communities are paving over the land at a rate that far outstrips actual population growth, sewage treatment plants are often far below capacity to deal with this increased input. To prevent untreated human waste from backing up into basements and streets, these systems have evolved escape valves, or "combined sewer overflows," to allow excess wastewater to discharge into the nearest creek.

The Scajaquada Drain buried a problem in one neighborhood only to have it resurface downstream as a sewage lagoon in the city's central park. In response, a decade later, the city built another drain, the Delavan Drain, to intercept the buried creek before it could resurface, and carry it all the way to the sewage treatment plant on the Niagara River. However, the old natural bed of the creek—through the cemetery, through the neighborhoods, under the expressway, and over to the river—was retained, as a *combined sewer overflow*.

Imagine it this way. Scajaquada, bearing its load of storm and sewer overflow from upstream suburbs, runs through an underground tunnel into the central city. Here, a hole in the tunnel dumps this mix into a smaller pipeline, the Delavan Drain, which carries it off to the treatment plant. In a sense, that is the end of Scajaquada Creek. However, when upstream areas flood or when the connection between the two drains is clogged, the creek, now officially a sewer, overflows into its old route through the city.

This led to another major engineering project in the 1970s that drained, dredged, and separated Gala Water (now Hoyt Lake) from its offending parent creek. However, the creek still can overflow into the lake and does so with increasing frequency as development spreads on its upstream floodplain.

But there is another factor in this equation. Underlying the cemetery, according to the grounds supervisor, is a "huge underground lake," with over thirty springs feeding the ponds and reflecting pools. These springs recharge Scajaquada Creek, restoring its flow downstream from the Delavan Drain diversion.

Jubilee Spring, the city's original water supply, originates in this sand and gravel aquifer. Three years after the 1832 cholera pandemic— the cholera bacterium, along with numerous other invasive species, had traveled to Buffalo and other towns across New York State by way of the newly completed Erie Canal[6]—Jubilee Spring Water Works began distributing this groundwater through 16 miles of hollow logs. Over the next decades, they extended the wooden pipes south to ever-larger cisterns under downtown Buffalo until the late 1890s, when Buffalo switched (mainly for firefighting) to the larger volume supply that could be pumped from Lake Erie. The Jubilee Spring Water Company continued to sell its waters in bottles through the 1920s, advertising it as "the only spring water in this part of the state with a certified seal," not only safe from fecal bacteria, but also "a known remedy for acid stomach, gout and rheumatism."

Although one cannot help wondering how 142,000 burials—half the living population of the city—affect this aquifer, Scajaquada appears mostly to benefit. After its brief breath of oxygen at the falls and plumped up by the springs, the creek meanders through the cemetery in a picturesque but oversized rock channel. Here are ducks, geese, raccoons, muskrats; even the occasional trout or walleye makes its way up to "Serenity Falls" from the Niagara River. But here too a strain of "Type C" botulism periodically kills off the wildlife, reminding everyone that Scajaquada is, after all, still a sewer.

Our Service is Second to None

JUBILEE SPRING WATER

It is important to know that this is a CERTIFIED Water

This water has supplied the citizens of Buffalo for over fifty years. It is bottled at the most sanitary plant in New York State. It has been tested by our leading chemists, Dr. Sy and Dr. Hill, and bacteriologist, Dr. Bentz, and pronounced as perfect as water can be. It is a known remedy for acid stomach, gout and rheumatism. It is certified daily, giving it the distinction of being the only spring water in this part of the state with a certified seal. Our plant is located in the center of the city and is open daily for inspection. This is the softest spring water in Buffalo.

Read the four convincing letters on 3rd and 4th pages of this folder

A TRIAL ORDER SOLICITED

FLOOD CONTROL

WALK IN THE densely developed neighborhoods of Cheektowaga and you will know—from the absolute flatness, the occasional sprawl of old black willows on a corner lot, the streets with names like Northcrest and Southcrest, and the long straight trenches running behind the backyards—that you are on a floodplain. However, you won't find the creek unless you really hunt for it.

Cheektowagans, if my car mechanic is any indication, don't like Scajaquada Creek. "What a joke," he says when I tell him of my interest. "They should put the whole thing underground." He remembers it choked with garbage. He remembers it flooding. He has nothing but contempt for the creek, hostility even, though the last major flood event was over forty years ago.

In the town of Cheektowaga, Scajaquada flooded enough to cause property damages in 1937, 1942, 1945, 1946, 1963, and 1967. Damages mounted in direct proportion to residential development in the floodplain. The more development, the more the Army Corps of Engineers' cost-benefit ratios warranted "channel improvements," which led to a major flood control project on Scajaquada in the 1970s. The project rerouted 5 miles of aquatic ecosystem into a grid of oversized ditches, cut four hundred large shade trees, and stripped all the other vegetation from the floodplain.

Flood control encouraged yet more development, including, in the late 1980s, a 1.4-million-square-foot shopping mall, which took over 65 percent of the creek's remaining floodplain and part of the creek itself. The proposal for the Galleria Mall on a site officially reserved in the town plan for flood prevention and wildlife habitat generated an environmental impact statement the size of two telephone books. But, in the end, the town decided that nothing would be lost that couldn't be mitigated. The question of wet weather runoff to sewers and consequent flooding and pollution downstream was answered with stormwater detention basins: vast rubbish-collecting wastelands encircled by the highway ramps to the mall. The question of wildlife habitat was answered with the developer's agreement to replace it somewhere else and, de facto, by the fact that many of the deer and other animals living on the site were killed on the highway during construction.

We find Scajaquada going down behind the Galleria parking ramp and resurfacing piecemeal through several parking lot drains on the other side of the mall, its water as steaming and brown as a hot cup of coffee.

THE SOURCE

ON MY MAP, the thin blue line of Scajaquada starts east of Buffalo, in the second ring suburb of Lancaster, and runs almost due west, to the Niagara River. Driving there, we see a land use pattern now familiar throughout the Great Lakes region, sometimes called the "sprawl of stagnation." While total population in Erie and Niagara counties has decreased over the past three decades, the urbanized area has tripled.[7] Scajaquada Creek is the central axis of the sprawl that has drained the urban core of over half its people.

Near where the map's blue line begins, we spot a billboard announcing the future site of 209 "estates," and a recently bulldozed track into a wetland. We follow the track in to where there's enough water flowing in tractor ruts to suggest that *this was the creek.*

Feeding this wash is a spring: a depression in the earth, maybe a foot in diameter and 10 inches deep, with fine sands at the bottom pulsing and bubbling like oatmeal boiling in a pot. Cold, crystal clear water overflows the brim. We can feel, deep in the spring's bottom sands, the mysterious heartbeat of underground forces—the birth pulse of young Scajaquada. It is the first spring I've ever seen bubbling straight from the ground and it is breathtaking, surrounded by its own micro-ecosystem of tiny plants and snails. The aquatic species that live here may exist nowhere else on earth. Headwater springs play an irreplaceable role in their contribution to biodiversity since the abundant species they host often have small geographic ranges and therefore, over time, survive based on their adaptation to local conditions.[8]

We are trespassing, nervous about the backhoe tearing out the vegetation upstream, working its way toward us. We go home to phone the state Department of Environmental Conservation and find out what is going on. In theory, this area should be protected by environmental regulations. In fact, it turns out, the developer has obtained all the necessary permits. Although the state Stream Protection Act says there shall be no disturbance to the creek's bed or banks, one permit allows a sewer pipe to be trenched under the creek connecting the subdivision down to the highway trunkline. In the engineering drawings, this looks like a perfectly reasonable operation. The other permit allows filling 3.8 acres of federally protected wetland, to be "mitigated" by the creation of a wetland elsewhere amid the 90 acres of new houses, pavement, and chemically treated lawns.

We finally persuade an environmental enforcement officer to go out and look at what is happening to the source of Scajaquada Creek. He calls back to say, yes, it is possible a permit has been violated, but, since he has no proof of what the site looked like before, there is nothing he can do now that would stand up in court. He further offers that Scajaquada is disturbed along that whole stretch—crossed by utility lines, culverted under driveways, and so on, implying "Why make a stink about this? The whole creek is a mess."

We ask him if he saw the spring.

He says no.

WHAT'S IN A NAME?

AT THIS POINT, we can sum up the story of Scajaquada Creek in seven words: "It was ruled the creek must go." Such was the thinking that turned it, like so many other urban creeks and rivers, into a sewer. Yet under the expressway, below the mall, beneath city and suburban neighborhoods, the creek survives.

At annual cleanups, the Parkside Greens fly a banner: "Free Scajaquada Creek Imprisoned Underground." It's a quixotic gesture, not unlike the creek itself coughing up a clear spring or a pair of beaver now and then. We might begin with more modest goals, like resolving some of the many mysteries our brief trip up the creek unearthed. What exactly was that black rock, for example, and where is its root? What is going on, hydrologically speaking, in the hyporheic zone below the cemetery? What was that 3-foot living crab doing embedded in the streambank?

And what about that name?

3.4. PARKSIDE GREENS' BANNER

We could begin there.

Sca-já-qua-da, says Seneca ethnologist Arthur Parker, is "one of the oldest string of syllables still spoken on the Niagara Frontier." Over seventy-five variations in the historical records—Scajaquada, Conjockety, Skendauchguaty, Scoijoiquoides, Scoy, and so on—evoke a multitude of new tongues grappling with the exotic indigenous word. "The earliest Kenjockety of whom we have clear record was known to Buffalo's first settlers as John," writes Parker. "He claimed, and his Indian neighbors acknowledged, that he was no Seneca, but a Kah-kwah [Neutral], his ancestors since 1650–51 presumably having lived with their Seneca conquerors."[9] Grandson of "the last survivor of the Neutral Nation," John Scan-dyuh-gwa-deh was adopted into the Seneca Nation and eventually became an influential chief. His own "family wigwams" were located on the north bank of his namesake creek, near the Niagara River, away from the Seneca territory at Buffalo Creek, closer to the ancestral territory of Jikonsahseh.

The name itself, says Orasmus Marshall, means "beyond the multitude." It was not the Seneca name for the creek. That was *Ga-noh'-gwaht-geh,* "after a peculiar kind of wild grass, that grew near its borders."

What kind of wild grass? The next reading—when the community rules "The creek must return"—might begin with that.

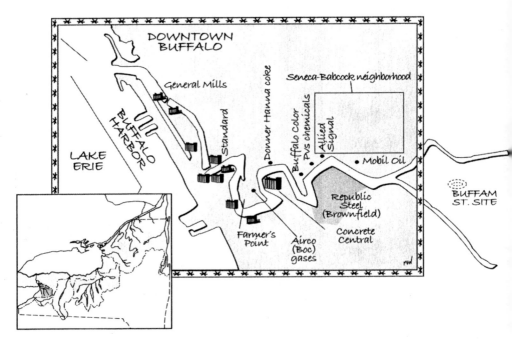

4.1. BUFFALO RIVER AREA OF CONCERN

FOUR

BUFFALO RIVER ABANDONED

> We are concerned about the confusion that descends on the
> community with every accidental release or explosion.
> Should we stay in our houses or evacuate? Who should we
> call? What should we do? Where should we go?
> —Seneca-Babcock resident's testimony
> to Buffalo Common Council, 1994

AUGUST 1982. We put in near the mouth of the river using the loading
zone of the General Mills puffed wheat and puffed rice factory. A man
who looks like Jack Nicholson, only puffier, comes out to watch us
wrestle the canoe off the top of the Toyota and lug it down the concrete bank to the river.

"You better move that car," he growls as we pass him on the return
trip for our gear.

Meanwhile, a very large security guard ambles over and says in a
surprisingly high, strangled voice that it's okay with him wherever we
park, but, just to be safe, better to leave the car on Ganson Street. So we
do.

We walk back single file to the red cedar canoe—Neil with the
paddles and life jackets, me with camera, lunch, and a road map—past
four or five guys who've come out for a smoke and a look at this
strange little procession through their morning shift. We load up, climb
in, and shove off, heading east up the river.

In the Great Lakes region, the molted structures left by a century of "heavy industry" (the messy work of turning huge amounts of raw material into basic building blocks like steel, oil, and flour) tend to be large and impressive, nowhere more so than along the last few miles of the Buffalo River as it meanders toward Lake Erie. Republic Steel, Donner Hanna Coke, Allied Chemicals, Buffalo Color, Mobil Oil, Huron Cement, Cargill, and their several precursors designed this landscape with the help of the many agencies who supplied the railroads, lift bridges and canals, and who dredged this naturally wide, shallow, meandering river into a deep navigable trench. Most of the private concerns—including the coke, steel, oil, and over half of the grain companies—have either shut down or regrouped and moved their production elsewhere. Their cast-off exoskeletons stand empty: coke ovens, blast furnaces, cooling towers, and rows of concrete grain silos whose once movable "legs" now rust in their tracks along the river's edge. They memorialize a time past or soon passing: the Iron Age, the Oil Age, Buffalo's own boomtown days as a major inland port.

Neither one of us is what you'd call an expert paddler. I ply mine a little too fast and loose, from time to time splashing Neil, who prefers not to be touched by the brown, oily water.

"Watch it!," he keeps saying testily.

He steers us too close to shore, where submerged pilings could rip or capsize our canoe.

"Can't you steer?," I say, equally fearful of contact with the water. "Don't blame me if we tip."

On our right we pass a quarter-mile or so of empty grain elevators fronted by wharves crumbling into the water. Buffalo's fireboat, the *Edward M. Cotter*, is the only vessel docked here, reminding us that sections of the river have caught fire in the past. On our left a long row of wooden warehouses lie burst at the seams, every window broken, in tall fields of Queen Anne's lace, Joe-pye weed, and oxeye daisies. Although the Environmental Protection Agency has recently reported the river's sediments to be "irredeemably saturated with toxic chemicals," its banks look to be recovering. An acre of sunflowers blazes across from the fireboat.

Our sense of the river as poisonous has made us edgy. Falling in would not be good, given the high fecal coliform counts from sewage overflows. However, as far as toxic chemicals go, our greatest risk would be from eating the fish. The next two decades of monitoring will reveal tumors and other deformities in 37 percent of Buffalo River fish. Even by 2004, the river will score "Poor" to "Very Poor" on an "Index of Biotic Integrity."[1] Up to 50 percent of the lower river's few species of pollution-tolerant bottom-dwelling invertebrates show deformities likely caused by polyaromatic hydrocarbons (PAHs) from coking operations. Sediment cores will show that contaminant concentrations peak at a depth of 6 feet. The relative depth and intensity of signature waste products reveal not only the species of industry that have inhabited the river but also the rises and falls in their productivity over the last century. Concentrations of chemicals and metals are highest at the river's edges and turning basins, places less disturbed by the routine dredging that keeps the main channel navigable.

We are not here to fish, nor would we probably eat one if someone were to hand us their catch-of-the-day. But people do eat fish from this river, especially people from the surrounding neighborhoods, the resident labor pool for industries that have since moved on.

"PLACE OF THE BASSWOODS"

DOWNTOWN BUFFALO'S skyline looms behind us, yet we could not be in more remote a spot. It is a place that has been abandoned before. Archaeologists have excavated five prehistoric (before European contact) Iroquoian settlements in this watershed dating back at least to 1500 and deserted some time in the mid-1600s. By most accounts, the inhabitants were Wenros, relatives of the Haudenosaunee, whom the Seneca Nation pushed out in order to gain further control as middlemen in the fur trade between the tribes further west and the markets to the east. The "Beaver Wars," fueled by the demands of European fashion, are said to have driven the Haudenosaunee to attack their relatives around the Great Lakes, resulting in the virtual destruction of the Wenros, Eries, Neutrals, and Hurons as separate nations between 1641 and 1657. According to this economic model for the river's depopulation, European mercantilism supplanted Indian trade patterns.[2] Competition in a global market for a high-demand, limited resource fostered increasing externalization of costs to "labor," to the environment, and finally to the resource itself. Once the beaver played out, the region was left, literally, to the wolves. How curiously this prefigures the scenario we witness some 350 years later as we canoe through a riverscape raw and disrupted by its recent abandonment.

What we know of pre-Seneca inhabitants on the Buffalo River we know mainly from the wastes they left behind. An earth wall encircled the westernmost village, known to archaeologists as the "Buffam Street site," part of which is now preserved in "Seneca Indian Park." It contained a trash pile 30 feet in diameter and 4 feet deep whose size indicates a long period of settlement and whose contents, like the sediment cores, tell us something about the people and the nature of their activities here:

> The refuse heap . . . was composed of layers and lenses of almost pure gray ashes alternating with a peculiar black, greasy carbonaceous earth . . . corn was abundant and its large size and great quantity gave sufficient evidence of the agricultural skill of the villagers. Beans and squash seeds attested their dependence upon the "Three Great Ones." With these were nuts and wild fruits, acorns, hickorynuts and walnuts and seeds of various berries.
>
> Bones of deer and bear were most numerous. Elk was represented together with wolf, dog and fox, wild-cat, raccoon, squirrel and rabbit. Bones of fishes of several species; of frogs and turtles; and the shells of fresh water mussels were abundant enough to show that the villagers derived much of their food from the nearby creeks and lakes.[3]

For all this abundance of game and good soil, it seems strange that after these villagers were gone, the river was not resettled for another 140 years. According to one historian, "there grew up around the abandoned village with its ruined fortifications a tradition setting it aside as a sacred place, a monument to the might of the Seneca."[4] This interpretation is reinforced by Henry Schoolcraft's discovery of an ancient mound within the earthwork, suggesting its use as a sacred place thousands of years earlier.

More recently, scholars have considered another factor in the Seneca wars that may further explain the long silence on the river. Smallpox swept through Haudenosaunee territory in 1634 and is said to have killed at least half the population in three months. By this hypothesis, the Seneca attacks on their neighbors were driven in part by the need to replace their massive losses caused by this epidemic.[5] With populations drastically thinned by war and disease, there may have been few people left to reinhabit the Buffalo River.

It was not until 1780, after the Western Campaign of the Revolutionary War destroyed Haudenosaunee villages across New York State, that refugees of the Seneca and other nations of the confederacy relocated here. The 1797 Big Tree Treaty established twelve reservations in western New York, including the 85,557-acre Buffalo Creek Reservation. Farmer's Brother, Red Jacket and Mary Jemison, "the white woman of the Genesee," were among those who eventually came to live and die here. They chose as their burial ground the very site of the prehistoric village overlaying the ancient mound. Haudenosaunee people still commemorate this spot—Seneca Indian Park at the foot of Buffam Street in South Buffalo—with stone monuments and occasional ceremonies.

Do-sho-weh, the Senecas' name for the river, evokes the uncanny quiet of a place where, in the late 1700s, the hum of bees once could be heard for miles.

> At the time of arrival of the Senecas, the striking feature of this locality was the predominance of the linden or basswood over all the other trees of the forest. They fringed both borders of the creek, and spread their foliage over its fertile bottoms. Seneca tradition tells us, that in the season when the tree was in flower, the hunting parties of the Genesee could hear, ere they reached the creek, the hum of the bee, as it gathered, in countless swarms, its winter stores from the abundant blossoms . . . The Senecas . . . seized upon this marked peculiarity of the place, and called it Dó-sho-wă . . . meaning, The place of the basswoods.[6]

"PAIN IS IN OUR HEARTS"

AT THE OHIO STREET BRIDGE, the Buffalo River takes a sharp left turn. Rows of grain silos crowd close to the banks on both sides, cutting off the sun and most of the sky. Fermented grain flushed from the steeping vats of American Malting floats on the water smelling of cow pasture. Our canoe startles a thriving colony of pigeons from their roosts under the bridge.

On the left, the *Ernest R. Breech*, an inauspiciously named laker as long and deserted as a downtown city block, loads grain into the Standard Elevator. A few men loitering at the railings wave as we paddle by. A stout handsome woman in a dark green business suit walks diagonally across the high sunlit deck holding a clipboard, like a stage director preoccupied with the next scene. She doesn't notice our canoe slipping by in the wings.

The three elevators on the right—Cargill, American, Lake & Rail—also show some vital signs. A lightbulb shines in the blackness beyond one open door. A six-pack of Coors, slung in a white T-shirt, hangs from one piling just below water level. We paddle through the

4.2. THE *BREECH* UNLOADS.

shadows, noticing the cracks in the concrete silos. The current picks up with the wind in the tunnel.

If this were 1800, we would now be crossing the border into the Buffalo Creek Reservation and approaching the first Seneca cabin, the home of *Hon-na-ye-was* or Farmer's Brother. Some maps still label the hammertoe shape of land around which the river makes a U-turn as "Farmer's Point." In 1795, a Seneca delegation from the Buffalo Creek territory walked to Philadelphia to meet with the new nation's president, known as *Destroys Towns* (see chapter 5), concerning the losses of land they had suffered through treaties they said were unauthorized and illegal. Washington responded by urging them to be content with less land, to forsake war and hunting, to take up instead the more settled and land-intensive business of farming. He himself, *Destroys Towns* said to his brother *Hon-na-ye-was*, was first and foremost a farmer. Farmer's Brother took the offered name, but he is remembered most for his exploits as a warrior. He led a pan-Indian resistance against British control of key Great Lakes interior posts in the Devil's Hole massacre of 1763 and, though in his eighties, he would lead them again on the side of the Americans in the War of 1812.

With the completion of the Erie Canal in 1825, pressures on the Seneca for their Buffalo Creek lands intensified. In 1827, they appealed again to the president, John Quincy Adams, claiming they had been "deluded and defrauded" into selling about a third of the reservation. "Pain is in our hearts in consequence of misconduct of some of the white people in attempting to get from us our land and our homes."[7] In 1838, they sold their remaining reservations in western New York to the Ogden Land Company. An era of unparalleled bribery, legal maneuvering, and strife led up to this decision, including, in 1830, passage of the Indian Removal Act authorizing President Andrew Jackson to forcibly transfer eastern tribes to Indian territory in the West. The sale was accompanied by a treaty that granted the Six Nations land in Kansas and guaranteed federal provision of transportation, schools, churches, and other aid. However, after the U.S. Senate amended the treaty by striking these provisions, the Seneca refused to ratify it. In 1842, with the help of the Quakers and attorney Daniel Webster, they negotiated a compromise whereby the Senecas renounced their claims to Buffalo Creek, and the Ogden Land Company released its hold on the Allegheny and Cattaraugus territories. By 1844, the Buffalo Creek

Seneca began leaving. I have read somewhere that some of the last to go vandalized the coveted basswood forest by stripping the bark from the trees. This may be Buffalo's first urban legend, denoting the bitterness surrounding both the beginning and end of the Buffalo Creek Reservation.

As I write this, the Senecas are returning to the Buffalo River with the purchase of 9 acres for the "Seneca Buffalo Creek Casino." As controversial as this casino is—to taxpayers who object to the inclusion of a nontaxpaying sovereign nation in the city's midst, to antigambling activists, and to river restoration advocates—there is a sublime irony in this "homecoming," as the Seneca Nation's president has called it.

While the Senecas were leaving, a flood of newcomers began arriving, including Christian Metz, prophet and leader of a religious commune in Germany, who came to Buffalo Creek in 1842 and recognized it as the place in the wilderness God had promised his people. He renamed Do-sho-weh "Eben-ezer," or Hitherto the Lord hath helped us, and by the summer of 1843 had purchased 5,000 acres at $10 an acre. The Ebenezer Community of True Inspiration farmed and logged off the land in twenty years, then sold it off in parcels and moved to the Iowa River to found the new community of Amana, inspired makers of kitchen appliances.

GRAIN ELEVATORS DEAD AND ALIVE

A GREEN THICKET fringes the shore of Farmer's Point: blackberry, hawthorn, pincherry, and vibernum planted by berry-eating birds perched in the willows. We canoe closer to look for fish, but even at less than a foot deep the water is too murky to see through. Bales of rust-trimmed flattened cars glitter on the distant shore, across a wide bend in the river. As we round the point, the Airco Industrial Gas plant erupts with a deafening whoosh and a cloud of steam. We have been hearing that explosion for some time now and calculate that it comes at 15-minute intervals, a new voice on the river issuing from the compression process used in manufacturing liquid nitrogen and liquid oxygen.

The colossal ruin of Concrete Central looms ahead, looking much closer than it is we discover as we zigzag through the river's coils. Architects from all over the world have traveled here to admire the

4.3. BUFFALO RIVER, 1995. CONCRETE CENTRAL IS AT TOP CENTER. COURTESY OF PVS CHEMICAL SOLUTIONS, INC.

Buffalo River's collection of grain elevators, especially this one in its "solitary and desolate grandeur," as Reyner Banham describes it in his guide to Buffalo architecture. As archetypes for the form-follows-function school of designers, Concrete Central and its companions "have done almost as much as the Buffalo works of Wright and Sullivan to shape the progress of modern architecture."[8]

In 1842, Joseph Dart set up the world's first steam-powered mechanized grain elevator on the Buffalo River, using Oliver Evans's newly patented "marine leg," which revolutionized the industry and is a conspicuous feature on all Buffalo's elevators. I saw firsthand how this works thanks to Bob Brehm, a millwright at Lake & Rail, who had invited me on board *The William McGonagle* earlier that summer to watch them load.

First the men set up for "dipping," in which the elevator leg is lowered directly into the ship's hold and a revolving chain of buckets scoop up the grain and carry it to the top of the bins (silos). They had to move *The McGonagle* forward a few yards to position the hatch beneath the elevator leg, which required much shouting and hand signaling from one end of the long ship to the other. There were about twenty-five men in the boat crew and a few more from Lake & Rail. As they set the ropes, blocks, and tackle for the two large shovels that move back and forth through the grain pushing it toward the sucking leg, one man somehow got his legs caught between the ropes and there was more yelling. Had they not stopped the motor, Bob said, the ropes snapping into position could have cut off his legs. Another scooper waded hip-deep through the gold wheat buds and took his position between the ropes and shovels. His job was to turn the shovels right side up should they fall backwards. Buckets of grain began traveling up the leg faster than we could see. A weights' master located halfway up in the leg housing took samples of each bin's grain to send back to a Detroit lab where it was tested for rat hairs and turds and finally milled and baked into bread to ascertain quality.

It had taken *The McGonagle* four days to come from Detroit and would take her four and a half days going back light. (By car, the trip from Buffalo to Detroit is about four-and-a-half hours). She was one of a fleet of old lakers owned by George Steinbrenner, who also owns the New York Yankees. She brought in about 450,000 bushels of grain that day. Although there seemed to be considerable room for human error and accident, the ship itself was spotless—brass railings in the engine room polished to a gleam, tools mounted square on their pegboards. She seemed to be as well-oiled, neat, and lovingly tended as a hobby train.

"WHERE SHOULD WE GO? WHAT SHOULD WE DO?"

CONCRETE CENTRAL sits a few feet back from the riverbank, rooted in a field of teasel, milkweed, and wild wheat. The waist-high grass slants west in the wind. An elevator leg stands frozen in the foreground. We glimpse ragged patches of blue sky through the breaches in the silos as we rest our paddles and slowly drift by. Every now and then we hear a metallic clang coming from within, like the bell of a buoy off the foggy coast of Maine. Heavy metal objects lay half-buried in the tall grass: the barrel of a cement mixer, a circuit box, the armature of a crane. We collect specimen images with snapshots. Two sandpipers run nervously up and down the thin pebble beach as we drift by.

From under a lifted railroad bridge we can see the black girders of two more lift bridges, both up, in the river loops ahead.

Across the river is a Krazy Kat landscape of smokestacks, cooling towers, and tanks belonging to Buffalo Color, PVS Chemicals, and the now defunct Donner Hanna Coke, all driven by steelmaking. Separating iron from its ore required blast furnaces fueled by coke. Distilling coal into coke created coal tars, which could be processed into a mind-boggling array of products including dyes, pharmaceuticals, fiberglass, and automobile coatings. Buffalo Color used the coal tars to "put the blue in blue jeans" with synthetic indigo dye. PVS Chemicals manufactured sulfuric acid, consumed in large volumes to neutralize the caustic waste of the dye plant.

Jacob Schoellkopf came to the Buffalo River from Germany in 1843 and made a fortune in flour milling and leather tanning before forming, with his sons, the Schoellkopf Aniline and Chemical Works in 1879. The plant operated continuously since then as National Aniline, Allied Chemical, and finally as Buffalo Color, until 2003, when the company declared bankruptcy. By 1917, this plant produced over half the coal-tar dyestuffs used in the United States, and was the largest single source of industrial pollution on the river.[9]

The first step in making indigo involves a reaction between aniline, formaldehyde, and cyanide in the presence of alcohol to create a compound called PGK that then reacts with sodamide and caustic in a fusion process to yield indigo. By-products released to the environment include aniline, dimethyl-aniline, butadiene, ammonia, cyanide compounds, nickel compounds, methanol, formaldehyde, maleic anhydride, sulfuric acid, and acetone. Aniline is a highly toxic substance, especially when ingested or inhaled, affecting the blood's ability to carry oxygen. High exposure can cause depression of the central nervous system, a fall in blood pressure, cardiac arrhythmia, and death. Lower level long-term exposures to, for example, employees in aniline dye plants are linked to bladder tumors. Less severe exposures, such as to communities neighboring an aniline dye plant, can cause headaches, eye irritation, weakness, and irritability. Aniline and butadiene are probable carcinogens.

4.4. BUFFALO RIVER. 1951. DATA AVAILABLE FROM
U.S. GEOLOGICAL SURVEY/EROS. SIOUX FALLS. S.D.

In the first eight years of reporting under the national Toxic
Release Inventory, beginning in 1988, Buffalo Color's permitted and
"fugitive" (accidental) discharges of aniline, dimethyl-aniline, and butadiene per year were, on average: 64,500 pounds to the air, 5,600 pounds
to the river, and 228,650 pounds to Buffalo's wastewater treatment
plant. This averaging does not account for spikes, such as accidental air
releases of almost 70,000 pounds of butadiene in 1990. In 1991, Buffalo
Color and PVS Chemicals together reported discharging over 570,000
pounds of toxics to the air.

In July 1991, people living in the Seneca-Babcock neighborhood,
then ranked eighth in the nation for industrial releases of cancer-caus-
ing substances, woke up to find a fine white powder covering their
cars, lawns, and houses. The plants in their gardens were dead along
with pet birds in cages near windows and fish in their aquariums. Dawn
Caldarelli and Marie Grable—two young mothers who, by asking questions, had become point people for such events in the neighborhood—
were besieged by residents wanting to know what it was and what they

should do. Eventually, they tracked it to PVS Chemicals, a block away, where an equipment malfunction had allowed over 14,000 pounds of sulfur dioxide to escape and shower the area with sulfuric acid.

Just like in the movies, an angry mob of Seneca-Babcock residents descended on city hall, demanding better protection. In response, the Buffalo Common Council issued a resolution declaring the Buffalo River a "Toxic Free Zone" and pledged to set up a Good Neighbor Committee to work with companies on the river to reduce their use of toxic substances. As a board member of the Friends of the Buffalo River, I would serve on this committee, along with half a dozen other community residents and advocates, over the next six years.

We spent most of this time receiving presentations and tours from the plant managers, learning about dye and acid-making, and being sensitized to the economic pressures of the global market. Buffalo Color, for example, was "at war with China," the world's leading indigo dye manufacturer, whose market share was growing, in large part, because China did not have the environmental protections and labor laws that drive up the costs of production in the United States. We spent the remaining time arguing over the purpose of the meetings. The Good Neighbor Committee understood this to be pollution prevention and invited in experts to discuss the possibilities of environmental audits to identify possible substitutes for toxic materials and processes. The companies countered with more presentations on measures already taken under the chemical industry's Responsible Care Program and through their own internal audits.

Meanwhile, accidental releases and spills continued, including, on July 12, 1994, a midnight explosion that blew out all the windows of the nearby Allied-Signal research facility and brought the neighbors back to city hall. "We are concerned about the confusion that descends on the community with every accidental release or explosion," they testified before the Common Council. "Should we stay in our houses or evacuate? Who should we call? What should we do? Where should we go?"[10]

In the end, this was what the companies responded to. They set up a Community Alert Network, a computerized telephone system to warn people, in case of an accidental release, to stay in the house and shut all the windows until further notice.

"GET THAT CANOE OUT OF HERE, YOU IDIOTS!"

THE CANOE BEGINS to hum like the steadily bowed string of a cello. Above the willows, the nose of *The Buffalo* moves slowly into view. It fills the bend in the river, then stops to realign itself. The stern swings out and the ship comes on at a glacial pace. About 6 miles of river, from the mouth up to the Mobil Oil tank farm, has been dredged to a depth of 21 feet, most of that cut through bedrock. *The Buffalo*, sitting low in the water, is duly cautious. Two men—one at the prow, the other, a long block away on the bridge—navigate through walkie-talkies.

Our canoe sings louder, amplifying the thrum of the ship's screw. *The Buffalo* blows her horn. We paddle frantically to get out of the way, but seem to be paddling in place, caught in some kind of undertow. Yelling at each other, "Paddle harder! Paddle harder," we manage to break free of her gravitational field and finally beach on the narrow strand below Concrete Central. We watch *The Buffalo* pass. At her stern, in the hull below the cabin stack, a square open window frames the head and shoulders of a woman in a white nurse-like uniform looking out at us.

"Where are you going?" I holler.

"Cleveland," she yells back.

"What have you got?"

"Iron ore."

Then she yells something we can't make out.

Neil thinks she said, "Get that canoe out of here, you idiots!"

I nod and raise my fist in an "Onward!" sort of gesture to my fellow woman in this no-man's-land of the Buffalo River.

After the Civil War, with the extension of railroads up and down the country and the discovery of vast iron ore deposits in Michigan, Buffalo was ideally located for steelmaking. It had the lake connection to Michigan's ore, rail connection to Pennsylvania's coal, and native limestone for processing. The New York State Steel Company, later Republic Steel, set up on the Buffalo River in 1905, about the same time that Lackawanna Steel (now Bethlehem) began production in its sprawling showcase facility on the lakeshore. By the 1920s, Buffalo was the second largest steel producer in the nation.

Directly ahead of us (the river doglegs to the left) Republic's smokeless stacks extend in both directions as far as the eye can see. Wooden pilings and rubber bumpers sheath the banks. In the foreground, a small yellow earthmover lurches back and forth between pyramids of iron ore still waiting to be shipped elsewhere.

We let the current carry us into the elbow where I eat my sandwich and Neil throws his, piece by piece, into the water. A brown bullhead jumps clear of the surface, almost landing in his lap. It is our first sighting of life in the river, and we read it as a good sign. However, given the health data for this species in the river (over twenty years later 87 percent of brown bullheads sampled in the Buffalo River still show lesions, tumors, or deformities of some kind), this could have been a cry for help.

FRIENDS

I DID NOT KNOW IT THEN, but the Buffalo River had a friend, a volunteer "riverkeeper," who had worked steadily on its behalf for over half a century. This was Stan Spisiak, a jeweler by trade, who somehow got to President Lyndon Johnson in the mid-1960s and alerted him to contamination problems in the river and in Lake Erie.

> President Johnson was my guest for three-and-a-half-hours. I showed him a bucket of sludge from the Buffalo River and gave him a big spoon to stir it with.
>
> "Who's doing it?" he asked. "I'm listening."
>
> I told him the Corps was dumping dredge spoils all around Lake Erie; that there was sludge like this in fifteen harbors around the Lake.[11]

Johnson issued an Executive Order to stop dumping dredged materials in Lake Erie; Spisiak received a presidential award as a "Water Saver of the Nation."

In 1988, a group of local activists, many of whom had been involved in the Buffalo River Remedial Action Plan process, picked up the torch Stan had carried so long. The purpose of the Friends of the

4.5. N.Y. STATE SENATOR ROBERT F. KENNEDY. "WATER
SAVER" STAN SPISIAK. AND N.Y. CONGRESSMAN
RICHARD D. MCCARTHY ON THE BUFFALO RIVER. JUNE
17. 1965. COURTESY OF THE BUFFALO AND ERIE
COUNTY HISTORICAL SOCIETY.

Buffalo River was "to promote, preserve and restore the Buffalo River
and its neighborhoods through public education, planning and development review." They initiated a "Watershed Learning Project" in Buffalo
and upstream schools, for example, and developed a greenway plan,

including a 100-foot setback for new nonwater dependent uses along the river that the City of Buffalo eventually passed into law. Eventually, the EPA awarded them a grant to take over New York State's function as "Remedial Action Plan" coordinator, which, as fate would have it, became the job of Stan's grandniece.

In 2002, the Friends added the all-but-orphaned Niagara River to their care, and in the following years led a coalition of groups in the Niagara hydropower plant relicensing negotiations with the New York Power Authority. In 2005, the Friends of the Buffalo Niagara Rivers joined dozens of other organizations around the Great Lakes to become part of Robert F. Kennedy Jr.'s growing Waterkeeper Alliance.[12] The new name—Buffalo Niagara Riverkeeper—reflects a change in mandate toward closer monitoring of activities on the two rivers and enforcement, through litigation if necessary, of environmental regulations.

Since Neil's and my first trip up the river, the New York State Department of Environmental Conservation has created a Buffalo River Urban Canoe Trail, with launching docks and even a guide map pointing out many of the local places I've mentioned along with typical sites: "Disturbed Shoreline," "Debris Bank," "Hobo Jungle."

It is still an edgy kind of experience, paddling up the Buffalo River, but I highly recommend it.

INTERLUDE

The Power of Water

OCTOBER 8, 1992. We are walking from the school to the river, waders
and fishnets in hand, trying not to look too self-conscious under the
direction of the *National Geographic* film crew. Our small parade—seventeen sixth graders (the River Rats), teacher Margaret Heaney, a few
Friends of the Buffalo River, followed by the director and cameramen—
marches past the Valley Community Center, around the pond, and over
the berm to the river now sparkling in early morning sunlight. A soft
breeze carries the sweet scent of aniline down from Buffalo Color
mixed with a hint of toasted grain floating up from General Mills.

National Geographic is doing a segment on the River Rats and our
"watershed learning project" as one of five stories it will feature in a
television special on American rivers: "The Power of Water." This is the
highlight: kids out on the Buffalo River collecting local species for a
classroom aquarium, part of the new science curriculum emphasis on
ecology. *National Geographic* intends to feature our river as their most
hopeful story. Buffalo's revival. Local television crews are also on hand
to capture this watershed moment in the city's history.

I walk in dread of what's going to happen next. Yesterday I was on
the river with Brian Shero, an aquatic limnologist, and Sally Uzunov, an
outdoor educator from nearby Tifft Nature Preserve. We spent the day
trolling these waters for fish or any other sign of aquatic life and found
none except two bloodworms that didn't look all that healthy.

At the river the students perch on a fallen willow while Allan
Jamieson, a Cayuga faithkeeper from the Six Nations Reserve in
Ontario, tells about the moving of the Haudenosaunee council fire to
Buffalo Creek after the scorched earth campaign of 1779, and about the

river's perseverance through its own time of burning. We give thanks to the water for all the life it sustains.

Then their teacher, the steady and indomitable Ms. Margaret Heaney, hands out waders, rubber gloves, fishnets, and pails and lets the kids go.

In no time at all, Joey catches a small yellow perch. Then Valerie gets a little bass, Danielle a minnow. By and by everyone catches something and the excitement spreads to the film crew, now hip deep in the river amid the stalking and splashing. The kids forget they are being filmed. They're coming up with bullheads, pumpkinseeds, emerald shiners, backswimmers, dragonfly nymphs, snails, scuds, water beetles, water boatmen, waterpennies, duckweed, elodea, milfoil, and more to be identified. Each new discovery is duly marveled at and transferred carefully to the collecting buckets.

Back in the classroom the River Rats begin an inventory on the blackboard while the riverwater settles in the aquarium and the cameras roll. Then they transfer plants, fish, and invertebrates to their new temporary home. Ms. Heaney hands out journals in which the students can draw, record their observations, and ponder the ecosystem curriculum questions about energy and nutrient cycling, population dynamics, and food web relationships.

In November, I accompany a handful of students after school, minus the film crew, back to the river to let the creatures go. In our own private ceremony, we burn a little sage and give thanks to the living water.

PART II

BEGINNINGS

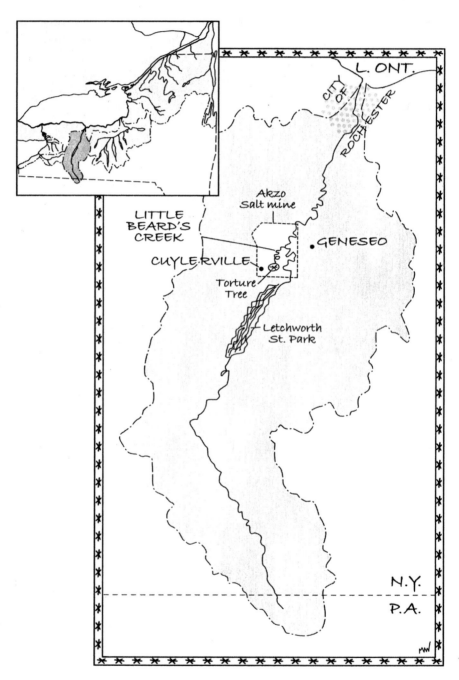

5.1. Genesee River Watershed

FIVE

GENESEE TORTURE TREE

Rereading Little Beard's Signs

> Look, I don't care
> how you interpret it.
> Every design to break the earth's skin
> deserves a couple of good tests,
> the deeper the better.
> You can say
> you're checking for soil
> structure, bedrock
> or groundwater,
> or you can admit
> that you wish
> to consult
> the gods down there.
>   —Stephen Lewandowski, "Test Pits"

MOST OF US HAVE PLACES on this earth that deeply resonate with who we are—because of some profound experience that took place there or perhaps for no reason we're aware of. One such spot for me is a little roadside park near the Genesee River, a half-mile from where my father's people settled and started a farm that eventually became a salt mine. A state historical marker indicates an oak tree on the edge of this site as the "Torture Tree," alluding to an old violence that has yet to be fully acknowledged and that continues to implode through the surrounding countryside.

OPENING THE WESTERN DOOR

SEVERAL HUNDRED MILLION years of geological history produced the particular beauty and abundance of the Genesee River valley. The unusually pure rock salt that has been mined there for a century comes from the Salina shales, formed in a climate and geography resembling that of Utah and Great Salt Lake over 400 million years ago. The deep alluvial soils of the Genesee floodplain tell us that the river itself in its present channel is old—very old. It was tributary to Lake Ontario when the lake was but a stream, and is said to be New York's only river that kept its northward course after the glaciers bent so many others east, west, or south.[1] Letchworth State Park—located along the Genesee's middle reach between its headwaters in Potter County, Pennsylvania (at 2500 feet above sea level), and its mouth in the City of Rochester on Lake Ontario (at 250 feet above sea level)—protects the river's deep gorge and three of its six spectacular waterfalls.

The Genesee valley long served as a boundary to colonial expansion into the Great Lakes region. "Western New York," the eight counties that lie west of the Genesee River, is a geopolitical division going back to the Revolutionary War, when the vast unexplored forest between the Genesee and Niagara rivers was the last Iroquois stronghold—the final frontier—preventing colonial expansion to the west. As late as 1755, the Genesee appeared on Great Lakes maps as a "river whose geography is unknown."

To the Haudenosaunee, Genesee country was the Western Door between the metaphorical Long House of the Confederacy (roughly the territory now called New York State) and the tribes and nations to the west. The Seneca Nation was its keeper. In his 1876 *A History of Livingston County New York*, Lockwood Doty describes over a dozen well-established Seneca villages near the Genesee at the time of the Revolutionary War—villages often named, according to the translations Doty uses, after the abundant and unusual water features of the region. *Dyu-non-dah-ga'-eh*, for example, the principal village and "home of the

5.2. SECTION OF 1755 MAP, "PARTIE OCCIDENTALE DE LA NOUVELLE FRANCE," BY M. BELLIN. COURTESY OF HISTORIC URBAN PLANS, INC., ITHACA, N.Y.

noted chieftain Little Beard," meant "steep hill creek," alluding to the Genesee tributary that descends a gully there, now called Little Beard's Creek. *Can-a-wau-gus* or "stinking water" was located near sulfur springs whose medicinal waters made the present-day village of Avon a fashionable resort destination and health spa in the nineteenth century. *Jo-nis-hi-yuh*, or "beautiful valley" was both a village and the Seneca name for the river.

What historians know of these precolonial settlements comes mainly from the letters and journals of the army that destroyed them in the 1779 "Western Campaign" near the end of the Revolutionary War. Volumes have been written on this campaign, one of the most controversial events in our nation's history, which, for the sake of my story, I will summarize briefly here.

Despite the Confederacy's attempt to maintain a policy of neutrality at the war's beginning, they gradually became engaged, and divided, forming alliances with either the Americans or the British as the best gamble for protecting their homelands. Many of the Senecas, Cayugas, Onondagas, and Mohawks joined the British in a series of raids against frontier pioneer settlements in eastern New York and Pennsylvania, centering on the Mohawk Valley, using British-held Fort Niagara as a stronghold and supply center.

The purpose of the Western Campaign, according to General George Washington's instructions to General John Sullivan, was to stop the raids and, if possible, "surprise the garrison on Niagara and the shipping on the lakes and put them into our possession." In terms of these objectives, the campaign failed. However, insofar as the underlying purpose was to open the Western Door, that is, remove the Haudenosaunee from their lands to make room for the new colonies, it was a stunning success. Washington outlined the "scorched earth" policy that would be key to that success in his May 31st orders to Sullivan:

> The immediate objects are the total destruction and devastation of their settlements . . . I would recommd. that some post in the center of Indian Country should be occupied with all expedition, with a sufficient quantity of provision; whence parties should be detached to lay waste all the settlements around, with instructions to do it in the most effectual manner; that the country may not be merely *overrun* but *destroyed*.[2]

Sullivan's principal target was Little Beard's village, near present-day Cuylerville, which he called "the Genesee Castle," believing it to be the capital of the "western Indians." He first saw it on September 14. Sullivan's journal record of his impressions are quoted in *A History of Livingston County*:

> We reached the castle or village, which consisted of one hundred and twenty-eight houses, mostly very large and elegant. The town was beautifully situated, almost encircled with a clear flat which extends for a number of miles where the most extensive fields of corn were, and every kind of vegetable that can be conceived.

By 3 P.M. the following day, Sullivan's army had destroyed Little Beard's village and burned the surrounding fields and orchards. He claimed to have destroyed forty villages, saying, "there is not a single town left in the country of the Five nations." In fact, a few survived including Conawagus, a few miles from Genesee Castle, which was not touched, according to one of the many Seneca accounts of *Destroys Towns'* ordered invasion.[3]

Sullivan and others who saw the Genesee River Valley in this conclusive campaign of the Revolutionary War described it as a kind of paradise, with its fertile soils, its seas of grass taller than a man, its fruit-laden orchards, and ears of corn up to 2 feet long. Their reports led to quick occupation after Indian removal. Or, as the Livingston County historian summarized a hundred years later, "Thus did the Indian campaign of 1779 directly lead to the settlement of the Genesee country; while the bloody wrongs inflicted by the aboriginal lords resulted in their expulsion therefrom, and their speedy downfall as a separate nation."

So went the official history.

BEHIND THE SIGN

I REMEMBER very clearly it was a hot summer day, mid-afternoon, every dip in the road ahead a dazzling mirage of water. We slowed down for a blue and gold state historical marker. It said: "Torture Tree." I was about ten years old. The sign is still there.

5.3. STATE HISTORICAL SIGN AT THE "TORTURE TREE"

It was a quiet country road in Livingston County, and this was a small clearing with a picnic bench, a flagpole, a giant old tree, and a strip of woods running along behind. Another sign stood near the tree. My parents and I must have wandered around the clearing, my father might have looked out across the road, across the cornfield, and up to the ridge dominated by the profile of a barn, long abandoned, built by my grandfather and his brothers. We were probably on our way there, and then to Cuylerville/Leicester cemetery where my father's mother was recently buried. The day was so calm we could hear an occasional knocking coming from the direction of the barn—probably a shutter on the cupola banging in the breeze, my dad said.

Somehow I talked them into leaving me there while they went and did whatever they were going to do. I was fascinated by the fact that this was the very spot, here the very same tree on which a torture had taken place. As soon as the old blue Buick disappeared down the road, I walked stealthily over to the tree and studied the bark for nicks or signs of blood. I examined the ground all around. I reread the sign by the road and then the one by the tree:

THIS WAYSIDE SHRINE MARKS THE PLACE
WHERE ON SEPTEMBER 14, 1779
TWO YOUNG SOLDIERS OF THE REVOLUTION,
LIEUTENANT THOMAS BOYD
AND SERGEANT MICHAEL PARKER
MET DEATH UNDAUNTED IN THE LINE OF DUTY.
AFTER LINGERING TORTURE THEY MARKED
WITH THEIR BLOOD
THE WESTERN LIMIT IN THE STATE OF NEW YORK
OF THE GREAT STRUGGLE FOR AMERICAN FREEDOM.

At the back perimeter of the little clearing was a wet gully, maybe 20 feet deep, half-filled with junk that people from the farms hereabouts must've been tossing in for some time. I climbed down to see what I could find amid the broken bottles and dismembered furniture. The footing was slippery; I had to hop from one trash pile to the next to avoid the deep muck. I was hopping toward something brilliantly red when I heard laughter.

I looked around, saw nothing, squatted down to render myself invisible, and listened.

It was kids laughing and shouting—playing. Dogs barking. Women murmuring. Slowly, these sounds got louder and louder until they were more like wailing, like screaming.

Then I remembered the roadside sign had said something about an Indian town.

I was in it. In the town, in a mass grave, feet sinking deeper into the mud. A whole village of men, women, and children—a whole people, I thought—had been wiped out here.

This idea, formed on the backside of the roadside marker, turned out to be wrong and yet not wrong. Little Beard's people were not literally killed here. The Senecas were, in fact, so well aware of the movements of General Sullivan's army as it advanced across New York State that they played mind games on them, left their own signs. When the underequipped militia shot their starved horses, the Senecas lined their next day's route with the severed horse heads—thus the town of Horseheads in Chemung County. Before the armies reached the villages along the Genesee, Little Beard and his people fled west toward the British fort on the Niagara River, but not before leaving another gruesome sign: the disemboweled and beheaded bodies of two Yankee scouts, Thomas Boyd and Michael Parker. Says Mary Jemison, a white woman who was adopted by the Senecas and lived through these times, "Little Beard, in this as in all other scenes of cruelty that happened at his town, was master of ceremonies, and principal actor."[4]

Five thousand Iroquois and allied tribes uprooted from their lands by the 1779 Western Campaign ended up at Fort Niagara. Hundreds died of starvation, dysentery, and exposure during the following brutal winter's encampment there. But many went on to resettle at Buffalo Creek or at one of the other reservations established by the Treaty of Big Tree eighteen years later. The Haudenosaunee not only survived this first Trail of Tears (the episode of major dam building on their lands 180 years later is sometimes called the second), they managed to rebuild and maintain traditional ways, albeit on a fraction of their ancestral lands in New York State. Little Beard himself lived until 1806. "He proved friendly to the pioneers and was esteemed by them for his good faith," writes the Livingston County historian. "No Indian was better informed, none more sociable than he, and with none could an hour be more profitably spent."

However, one would never suspect this from the roadside markers. These compound the violence they commemorate by suggesting that the perpetrators were the inhabitants of the country, that they are gone, that the appropriation of land and resources following their removal was, in fact, western New York's contribution to "the great struggle for American freedom."

Thus is the stage set for part three in this ecohistorical drama.

UNDERMINING THE VALLEY

MY FATHER WAS BORN in Cuylerville, a country crossroads less than half a mile west of where Little Beard's village once stood and the Torture Tree still stands. His father, John Pinkerton Wooster, and two uncles were farmers there, together possessing 900 acres of the famous fertile bottomlands drained by Little Beard's Creek and the Genesee River. John Pinkerton's grandfather, William Ward Wooster, had bought the land some time back in the 1830s, and had moved his household from Duchess County by way of the Erie Canal and ox cart to this remote place only recently abandoned by Indians. William Ward must have heard about the place from his grandfather William, who was part of the Mohawk Valley prong of the Western Campaign under General James Clinton. Clinton's army joined forces with Sullivan's in Genesee country in late August 1779. By mid-September they were done, having destroyed Little Beard's castle along with *Jo-nis-he-yuh* and other Seneca towns along the river.

In the late 1890s, Sterling Salt Company bought the mineral rights below the family farm and sank a shaft, the "Barbara shaft," in John Pinkerton's backyard, a shaft extending down to the salt vein running 1,000 feet below the surface. That vein, according to my Uncle Wheelock, stretches from Syracuse, beneath Lake Erie, all the way to Detroit. John Pinkerton became a weights master in the salt mine. His wife, Gertrude Wheelock, cooked for the "New York bigwigs" as she called

5.4. WOOSTER BARN, CUYLERVILLE, N.Y.

them, and helped nurse the victims of assorted accidents in and around the mine. My cousins all left farming to take up salt mining.

Two icons center the family's stories and photos: the cathedral-like Wells Patent truss barn built by our grandfather and his brothers, and the old salt mine shaft that stood on the land for half a century after the mine was closed. As a child, I made many pilgrimages to these gigantic ruins with my parents. You could still find old horse collars and rusty hardware lying about.

By the 1930s, the Barbara shaft was closed and the International Salt Company had consolidated mining operations 4 miles north at Retsof. In 1969, the Dutch conglomerate Akzo Salt Inc. took over and enlarged the mine to 6,500 acres, the largest mine for road salt in North America, the second largest in the world. At some point Akzo acquired, along with the mineral rights, the *cavity rights*, so that once the salt was taken, profit could be made by using the empty space for waste disposal. By the 1980s, plans for burying waste incinerator ash in the mine had divided the Livingston County community between those

5.5. STERLING SALT MINE SHAFT.
CUYLERVILLE. N.Y.

who saw new jobs and those who saw the risks to surrounding groundwaters from the heavy metals and other toxins contained in municipal
incinerator ash.

In 1994, Akzo made national news, reaching a landmark $100 mil-
lion in sales of 10.5 million tons of salt to cities, towns, and counties
stocking up after the bitter winter of 1993. On March 12, 1994, an 800
by 600-foot section of 300-foot-thick ceiling collapsed near the deepest
section of the mine at Cuylerville under the old Barbara shaft. The collapse caused the limestone above to crack and breach the floor of an

underground reservoir of unknown but reportedly "almost infinite" capacity. This aquifer is below another deep soil aquifer, which is below the floodplain of Little Beard's Creek and the Genesee River. Water began draining into the mine at a rate of 24,000 gallons per minute.

John T. Boyd Co., a mining and geological consultant hired by the state to investigate the cave-in, blamed Akzo for its mining techniques, specifically for "pillar robbing" or mining into the salt pillar roof supports. "The principal cause of the mine collapse is the use of yield pillars in an area where solid rock cover is insufficiently thick to accommodate the formation of a wide arch," Boyd's experts concluded (Associated Press, August 29, 1995). Months before the actual cave-in, miners were reporting to management that cracks were forming in the roof and the caverns with small pillar supports were dropping by inches. According to one miner, "70 percent of the men raised concerns with the company about the design. They'd listen, and continue" (Rochester *Democrat and Chronicle*, April 24, 1994).

Accusations mounted with the evidence. However, there was no trial and there were no convictions. Instead the state attempted to save the mine by pumping millions of gallons of saltwater into the Genesee River. But the mine flooded anyway. "Mine becomes subterranean salt-water sea," read one *USA Today* headline. The honeycombed substrata continued to implode, poisoning private water wells with salt, barium, and methane gas. At a family reunion in 1995 my cousin gave me a handful of articles from local newspapers showing the growing radius of residents impacted by the mine disaster—miles beyond the epicenter of the collapse, which was below the old family farm. A 600-foot sinkhole developed over the site of Little Beard's town and the Torture Tree. The tree itself began to tilt ominously as the land around it filled with water. "The mood around here is tense," said the former town supervisor. "This community is dependent on the mine. On the other hand, a much larger community, one that stretches to Canada, is concerned about what the salt will do" (*The Buffalo News*, March 20, 1994).

In November 1994, just eight months after the collapse, state and county officials announced a $53-million incentive package for a new salt mine just across the Genesee River from the old one. This, despite a lawsuit filed by affected citizens citing "gross negligence" and despite the protests of geologists and environmentalists who cited poor to criminal management of the old mine. Representatives of the mining industry convinced state legislators that there was no need for a detailed review of the design and technology for the new mine because mining disasters are rare. A small group of Native Americans staged a protest at the new site, claiming construction would violate ancestral burial grounds. Archaeologists had been excavating an early Indian village there, though no gravesites had yet been identified. The new company, American Rock Salt, said it had no intention of doing any more archaeological studies.

Western New York's primary garbage disposal company, Integrated Waste Services, also filed for $700 million in damages and lost profits since the mine's collapse terminated the incinerator ash disposal project.[5] A citizens' group called PACE (Protect a Clean Environment) claimed that Akzo's increased extraction rates in the Cuylerville section of the mine were partially motivated by the desire for more cavity space for the anticipated waste. Their December 1994 newsletter, the *Genesee Valley Guardian,* warned that the new company required all deeds with landowners to sign over both mineral rights (the right to mine under their property) *and* the cavity rights. And so the threat persists.

FARMER AND ESSAYIST Wendell Berry once proposed that we adopt land use policies based on a worldview that acknowledges the true depth of our ignorance. His words describe the practice of "adaptive management," compensating for the limits of our ecological knowledge by proceeding incrementally, with small, reversible actions. [6]

> To call the unknown by its right name, "mystery," is to suggest that we better respect the possibility of a larger, unseen pattern that can be damaged or destroyed and, with it, the smaller patterns . . .
>
> If we are up against mystery, then we dare act only on the most modest assumptions. The modern scientific program has held that we must act on the basis of knowledge, which, because its effects are so manifestly large, we have assumed to be ample. But if we are up against mystery, then knowledge is relatively small, and the ancient program is the right one: Acting on the basis of ignorance, paradoxically, requires one to

know things, remember things—for instance, that failure is possible, that error is possible, that second chances are desirable (so don't risk everything on the first chance).[7]

I read the salt mine disaster along these lines. What happened under Little Beard's town revealed a larger, unseen pattern: the intricate structure of groundwater underlying and upholding the Genesee Valley. And it gave us something else—perhaps another sign from that trickster, Little Beard, whose town's collapse saved the valley, at least for now, from a toxic filling that could have affected its inhabitants, human and wild, for generations to come.

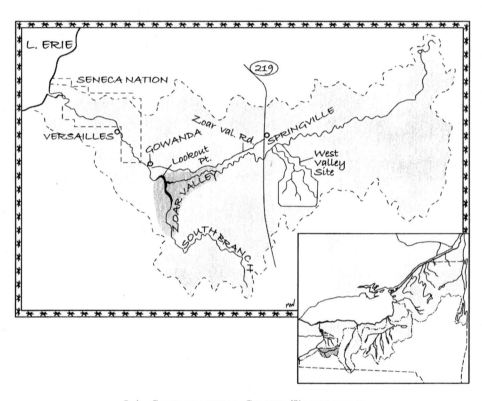

6.1. Cattaraugus Creek Watershed

SIX

ZOAR VALLEY GENESIS

Naked truth is a deep disguise which those accustomed to
deceive cannot often penetrate.
—Eber Russell, *Map of Ho-de-so-sau-nee-ga*

TAKE THE ZOAR VALLEY ROAD, following Cattaraugus Creek from
Springville to Gowanda. At its east end, it starts out normally enough, a
paved two-lane straightaway between farms and cornfields. But, after a
few miles, it begins to relax, its edges soften, it curves and curls with the
bends in the creek, nestled in the grasses of the floodplain. Like the
creek, the road seems to have carved its own path out of the landscape.
You slow down, you feel like waving to everybody you see—fat horses
knee-deep in ferns, tribes of Canada geese among the bulrushes,
columns of cattails blending into plantations of corn and hay. Halfway
to Gowanda there's a spring with a long thin pipe carrying its sweet-
scented stream to the road so you can take a dose home, like the other
pilgrims you'll meet there filling plastic jugs.

You are in the Zoar Valley, "the Grand Canyon of the East," a wide
steep-walled valley starting near Springville in southern Erie County,
narrowing to a 400-foot-deep gorge as it approaches Gowanda, 20
miles further west. From its headwaters in Wyoming County, 69-mile-
long Cattaraugus Creek flows west to Lake Erie. Its centerline forms
the boundary between Erie and Cattaraugus counties except in the last
11-mile stretch, where the counties retreat 3 miles on either side and

6.2. THE ZOAR VALLEY LOOKING TOWARD THE CONFLU-
ENCE OF CATTARAUGUS CREEK AND SOUTH BRANCH

the creek bisects another nation, a 21,680-acre territory belonging to the Seneca Nation of Indians.

Park your car in the clearing at the end of Valentine Flats Road and follow the unmarked but well-traveled trail northeast along a knife-edge ridge to Lookout Point. Cattaraugus Creek doglegs around you several hundred feet below, skirted by Valentine Flats, a forested flood-plain named after the family who once farmed here. Upstream a ragged profile in shale points the confluence of two deep canyons carved out by the main stream and the south branch of Cattaraugus Creek.

By national and state measures, this is the highest-quality watershed remaining in the lower Great Lakes, with the Zoar Valley "the largest area by far of intact landscape, old growth forest, and high quality head-water streams."[1] However, despite its primeval appearance, this is also a place of long-standing human presence. In fact, from Springville to Lake Erie, the Cattaraugus Valley harbors more relics of the earliest cultural history of this region than any other stretch of landscape I know. Native Americans have been here for ten centuries, perhaps long enough to have seen the Zoar when it was a mere crack in the Allegheny plateau. By contrast, European settlement—despite two centuries of logging, milling, farming, tanning, and dumping—seems to have come and gone. Two-hundred-year-old trees still tower from slopes too steep to log. Secondary forest has recovered thousands of acres. But this too is deceptive. Some legacies, like the ghostly trail of contaminants extending down Cattaraugus Creek from an upstream nuclear waste burial site, may mark this landscape for centuries to come.

From your perch at Lookout Point, note the scarred section of north wall half a mile upstream. Near the top, about 250 feet above the creekbed, you may see a small elongated shadow, black at the center. Locally known as "the Indian Cave," this dark trace is not a destination, but a point of reference for two very different cosmologies that overlay the Zoar Valley and this entire verdant, burnt-over part of the Great Lakes region.

ZOAR

AHAZ ALLEN first bestowed the name "Zoar" on a tiny flat of land on the south side of the valley in 1813, just twenty years after the Holland Land Company purchased 3.6 million acres west of the Genesee River and but sixteen years since Indian title to the land was extinguished at the Big Tree Council in 1797. With the name the ground shifted; this unknown frontier was suddenly linked into a Judeo-Christian frame of reference from half a world away.

"Zoar" is from the Book of Genesis, specifically from the story of Abraham and Lot who, like Ahaz, were looking for a new place to settle. "Then Abraham said to Lot . . . 'Is not the whole land before you? Separate yourself from me. If you take the left hand, then I will go to the right; or if you take the right hand, then I will go to the left.' And Lot lifted up his eyes, and saw that the Jordan valley was well watered everywhere like the garden of the Lord, like the land of Egypt, in the direction of Zo'ar."[2]

The direction of Zo'ar, however, also led to the sin city of Sodom, "where the men were wicked, great sinners against the Lord" (13:13), and which the Lord would obliterate, after bargaining first with Abraham, then with Lot. Abraham dealt for mercy if just ten right-minded men could be found in the valley, and lost. Lot bargained for a safe haven in the city of Zo'ar. "Behold, yonder city is near enough to flee to and it is a little one. Let me escape there—is it not a little one?—and my life will be saved!" (19:20)

The Lord spared Zo'ar and Lot, but not Lot's wife who turned back to see the brimstone and fire raining down on "all the valley, and all the inhabitants of the cities, and what grew on the ground." Abraham witnessed the scorched earth the next morning: "and lo, the smoke of the land went up like the smoke of a furnace." Lot, now afraid to live in the valley, even in the tiny protectorate of Zo'ar, retired to a cave in the hills, where his daughters contrived to sleep with him and beget sons who would father new lines of people.

My *Oxford Annotated Bible* explains this disturbing episode as "a memory of a catastrophe in remote times when seismic activity and the explosion of subterranean gases changed the face of the area," making a Dead Sea of the formerly fertile Jordan Valley. "Zoar," it says, means "small," and refers to a little town that survived the calamity at the southern end of the Dead Sea.

Ahaz Allen likely invoked the name Zoar in his own wager for safety and survival. However, with the name came a story reflecting a mind-set, a cosmology in which the surrounding valley, "well-watered everywhere like the garden of the lord," could justifiably be laid waste.

"MAP OF HO-DE-NO-SAU-NEE-GA"

I FIRST FOUND reference to a Haudenosaunee genesis story in relation to the Zoar Valley on a handmade map. At this time I was working for the Erie and Niagara Counties Regional Planning Board on wellhead protection outreach to the eleven municipalities left in these two counties whose water supply was not from Lake Erie or the Niagara River, but from underground sources.

In 1987, the U.S. Environmental Protection Agency designated the groundwater deposit underlying much of the Cattaraugus Creek watershed a "sole source aquifer"—one of just nine in New York State and the only one in western New York—a high-yield supply of ice contact water left by the receding glacier. The Cattaraugus Creek Basin Aquifer supplies villages and private wells across 35 miles of the glacier's terminal moraine system with better quality and far more affordable water than could be piped from Lake Erie. But it is also vulnerable to contamination. Under the Safe Drinking Water Act, projects over sole source aquifers require greater review in terms of their potential to pollute groundwater and it was my job to help local officials regulate land uses accordingly.

I had stopped at the Holland Land Company Museum in Batavia, thinking they might have old records that would aid the work of defining public water supply recharge areas where certain land uses like dumps, mines, gas, oil, or chemical storage should be prohibited. There, framed on the wall, was a large, hand-drawn, hand-colored "Indian map" of New York State with the following title block:

> Map of Ho-de-no-sau-nee-ga or the People of the Long House compiled 1851 by Lewis H. Morgan and Ely S. Parker, a Seneca Sachem, from several French maps of 1720 or earlier, showing ancient trails, lakes, villages and principal locations with their aboriginal names.

> Redrawn 1962 by Eber L. Russell, historian, Perrysburg, N.Y. with additions of villages, trails and springs from more than fifty years of research.

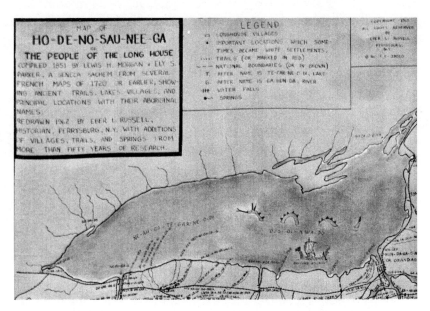

6.3. A PORTION OF THE "MAP OF HO-DE-NO-SAU-NEE-GA." COURTESY HOLLAND LAND OFFICE MUSEUM, BATAVIA, N.Y.

It was a completely water-oriented map, with creeks, springs, and watershed divides not only marked, but also illustrated by stories and legends noted in the margins, which took up fully a quarter of the map's space. One of these stories linked a local landmark—a cave—with a short narrative appearing under the heading "Mythology":

> Oat-gont, the Wizard of Gus-tan-go (Versailles) by trickery and deceit he overcame his victims and imprisoned them in a cave at the forks of Ga-da-ges-ga-o and Dju-na-ga-da-gus (Cattaraugus and South Branch). The cave is still there. He was finally beaten by a young man clad only in a breech cloth and moccasins, no paint or disguise . . . Out of this grew this 'saying of the wise ones' Naked truth is a deep disguise which those accustomed to deceive cannot often penetrate.

Where did this story come from? Since I could find no other reference to it in Lewis Morgan's 1851 book, *League of the Ho-de-no-saue-nee*, I turned to Eber Russell, whose collected papers are housed in the Patterson Library in the village of Westfield. Russell (1881–1966) was an engineer by trade, an archaeologist by natural bent, who spent much of his life digging for traces of early Iroquoian and pre-Iroquoian life in the Cattaraugus Valley and giving talks about his theories on the same. He was an expert on local history to his audiences; a pothunter to his disparagers. He was a member of the local Quaker Committee for Justice to the Indians, adopted into the Seneca Nation in 1925, and later recognized with a Peter Doctor Memorial citation for "distinguished service as a true advocate of Indian legend, tradition and history."

He tells of learning Seneca legends from Henry Thompson, said to be one of the few Senecas then remaining alive who could recount the ancient, unrecorded stories. Russell learned as well from his friend and fellow digger Arthur C. Parker, who became an archaeologist and ethnologist for the New York State Museum. "Arthur and I were within days of the same age, were interested in the same things, in many ways thought the same," says Russell.[3] Their friendship echoes the earlier collaboration of the map's originators, Seneca chief Ely Parker (grand uncle to Arthur) and Anglo anthropologist Lewis Morgan.

In *Seneca Myths and Folk Tales*, Arthur Parker relates the main elements of the wizard's cave myth to the Seneca creation story in which the daughter of Sky Woman gives birth to twin boys, Good Mind and Evil Mind, elsewhere called the right and left-handed twins, or Maple and Flint. As Parker tells it, their struggle culminates with a scene near the tree of life that Evil Mind has desecrated. For this transgression, Good Mind imprisons Evil Mind in a cave.

> Soon Good Mind slept again and was awakened by Evil Mind beating him with deer-horns, seeking to destroy him. They rushed inland to the foot of the tree and fought each other about it. Evil Mind was very fierce and rushed at his brother thrusting the horns at him and trying to pierce his chest, his face or tear his abdomen. Finally, Good Mind disarmed him, saying, "Look what you have done to the tree where Ancient One was wont to care for us, and whose branches have supplied us with food. See how you have torn this tree and stripped it of its valuable products. This tree was designed to support the life of men-beings and now you have injured it. I must banish you to the region of the great cave and you shall have the name of Destroyer."
>
> So saying he used his good power to overcome Evil Mind's otgont (evil power) and thrust him into the mouth of the cave, and with him all manner of enchanted beasts. There he placed the white buffalo, the poison beaver, the poison otter, snakes and many bewitched things that were otgont. So there to this day abides Evil Mind seeking to emerge, and his voice is heard giving orders.[4]

At the Seneca Nation library in Salamanca, I asked the librarian if there was any printed version of this story generally regarded as most authentic. She handed me a 1923 typescript entitled *Seneca Myths and Legends*, collected by Jeremiah Curtin for the Bureau of American Ethnology. This telling contains a twist evoking the map's 'saying of the wise ones'—"Naked truth is a deep disguise which those accustomed to deceive cannot often penetrate":

> Each knew somewhere in his mind what it was that was his own weak point. They talked about this as they contested in these duels, day after day, and somehow the deep mind of each

entered into the other. And the deep mind of the right-handed twin lied to his brother, and the deep mind of the left-handed twin told the truth.

On the last day of the duel, as they stood, they at last knew how the right-handed twin was to kill his brother. Each selected his weapon. The left-handed twin chose a mere stick that would do him no good. But the right-handed twin picked out the deer antler, and with one touch he destroyed his brother. And the left-handed twin died, but he died and he didn't die. The right-handed twin picked up the body and cast it off the edge of the earth. And some place below the world, the left-handed twin still lives and reigns.[5]

I had been looking for clues to the groundwater supply and had stumbled instead upon a series of Haudenosaunee stories about the ongoing creation of the world. Moreover, these stories touched down at a place on a map—a cave at the forks of Cattaraugus Creek and South Branch—a place still in the world. As Russell reminds us, *The cave is still there.*

I set out to find it.

THE NAKED GUYS

WE—my friend Suzanne, my twelve-year-old son Taylor, his friend Justin, and I—started at the Forty Bridge on South Branch, the only Zoar Valley access we knew of at the time. We figured if we walked downstream we'd eventually come to the fork with Cattaraugus Creek. It was Memorial Day, the end of a spring full of rain, and the water was high. We wandered downstream through the wooded gorge, which steepened until we found ourselves on a narrow shale ledge hugging the canyon wall to keep from falling into the roiling creek. Unable to proceed, unwilling to go back, we stalled awhile. The boys got interested in the dark two-lined salamanders nestled in the moist black cracks of the ledge. Suzanne leaned back for a smoke. I was scanning, half focused, the section of Canadaway shale in front of me for any fossilized patterns of life. Suzanne alerted me quietly.

"Is that a naked guy I see?" she said, looking down at her feet, gesturing with a slight thrust of her head.

It was. A dark and paunchy middle-aged man walked slowly on the path through the woods on the bank opposite. He took no notice of us. Four or five other naked people showed up, including one grandmotherly woman, walking like ghosts through the trees across the creek without seeming to notice us. We abandoned our search for the cave and headed back upstream. The boys were just as happy to return to the bridge, which was full enough of spent bullets to start a collection.

Back at the parking lot, a young state trooper was methodically ticketing cars for some infraction not apparent to us. We asked him how far it was to the confluence with Cattaraugus Creek.

"Did you see any naked guys?" he replied.

We looked at each other, unsure how to reply

"Well then," he grinned, "you were almost there." He explained it as a nudist colony that had been around for many years, bothering no one, perfectly harmless. He seemed remarkably tolerant for a cop writing tickets in the midst of a wilderness area, even taking the time to explain to the boys the different calibers of shells they had pried from the wooden body of the old bridge.

We later found that the designation of the forks as a "naturalist area" goes back to the 1800s; that even the Valentine family, who farmed the nearby flats in the early 1900s, allegedly included it in a clause to the deed when they sold the land. Given what we were looking for, this seemed auspicious. It was as if one element in the wizard's cave story, the naked hero, was weirdly in place, happily trumping the biblical brimstone that otherwise might have rained down upon the place.

ORIGINS

MANY GEOLOGISTS consider Zoar Valley to be postglacial and therefore of relatively recent origin. They connect its formation with the preglacial Allegheny River drainage, when the Allegheny, instead of looping south, flowed northwest through the Cattaraugus and Conewango valleys to ancestral Lake Erie. As the last glacier receded, the story goes, it left a moraine system across northern Cattaraugus County, preventing the Allegheny from finding its old route to Lake Erie. Now the Allegheny turns south to the Ohio and thence to the Mississippi, while the Cattaraugus, after cutting the Zoar, flows north-west to Lake Erie through the broad, open, preglacial valley of the ancestral Allegheny. South Branch, which joins the main stream just above the village of Gowanda, uses parts of the old Allegheny drainage.[6]

If people were here 10,000 years ago, as Eber Russell spent much of his life trying to prove, they were here before the Zoar Valley was formed. Current archaeological finds confirm this early presence of people in the Great Lakes region. Researchers have found projectile points near mastodon bones at a site in western New York that appears to have been a north–south migration corridor for large animals and the hunters who followed them[7] and mastodons are thought to have gone extinct at least 10,000 years ago. This view would not surprise the Seneca women I talked with at the Cattaraugus senior citizen apart-ments, who, when I asked how long the Senecas had lived on Cattarau-gus Creek, replied, "Forever."

What is so interesting here is the relative compression of major geologic events into a period that could have been witnessed, and influ-enced, by people. These timelines suggest a much more dynamic land-scape than we relative newcomers would suspect with our scant experi-ence of a few hundred years; they also suggest a continuum of local human experience that, quite literally, extends back to the valley's genesis.

WORKING AGAINST TIME

MY NEXT FEW TRIPS to the Cattaraugus Valley were with Ray Vaughan, a member of the Coalition on West Valley Nuclear Wastes, who was studying the riverbanks and bedrock outcrops upstream from the Zoar. Ray was looking for clues to the valley's underpinnings in support of the coalition's campaign to have a nuclear waste site cleaned up. In effect, the coalition was doing the work that the state should have done decades earlier, *before* leasing thousands of acres near the village of West Valley to a private corporation, Nuclear Fuel Services, for an ill-fated venture in radioactive fuel reprocessing.

Officially called "The Western New York Nuclear Service Center," the West Valley site lies within the watershed of Buttermilk Creek, a tributary feeding into Cattaraugus Creek 40 miles upstream from Lake Erie. Using its power of eminent domain, New York State purchased 3,300 acres of farmland in the early 1960s, hoping to position itself, in Governor Nelson Rockefeller's words, "at the forefront of the atomic industrial age now dawning." The general idea was for western New York to become a global center for reprocessing uranium and plutonium from spent fuel rods, supplied mainly by military and commercial atomic waste stockpiles, to fuel domestic nuclear power plants. Buffalo, just 35 miles north, was designated a nuclear port to receive radioactive wastes from around the world via the St. Lawrence Seaway. "The atomic age, rich in challenge and opportunity, stretches limitlessly into our future," said Governor Rockefeller, announcing the plan. How darkly prophetic those words would be.

Reaction in the farming community around the tiny village of West Valley was mixed, with many townsfolk welcoming the promised boom in new nuclear industries and jobs, while the farmers were given a rushed, take-it-or-lose-it deal averaging about $90 per acre for their land. Adding to their bitterness, they had to move off the land quickly, with little time to salvage anything from the farmhouses and barns, which were burned to the ground on a single Saturday. "The whole operation at West Valley was characterized by a remarkable degree of impatience," says coalition member Carol Mongerson in her history of the site.[8]

After start-up in the mid-1960s, the Western New York Nuclear Service Center saw just six years of actual processing of nuclear materials—most of it arriving from and returning to the Department of Defense atom bomb factory in Hanford, Washington. The "atoms for peace" and "sword to ploughshares" rhetoric surrounding the plant's start-up turned out to be as deceptive as the forecasted economic bonanza. By 1972, after discharging over five million gallons of liquid radioactive waste into local streams, the site at West Valley was on its way to becoming a massive problem that would take billions of dollars to remedy. In the mid-1970s, the plant was shut down, but the Nuclear Service Center was applying for a license to expand, at which point a group of citizens formed the Coalition on West Valley Nuclear Wastes and intervened in the licensing proceedings. In 1976, New York State withdrew its permit for stream discharges and the Nuclear Service Center abandoned the plant. This left the Cattaraugus Creek watershed with an *otgont* legacy: 600,000 gallons of high-level radioactive waste, 2.5 million cubic feet of buried low-level waste, and thousands of acres of land untaxed and unusable by area residents.

Since 1980, the U.S. Department of Energy has spent about $2 billion on processing the high-level waste into radioactive glass logs, which are expected to be removed from the site some day. But the buried waste remains a threat to surface and groundwater and all who depend on it.

WHEN I MET RAY, the coalition was studying the bedrock geology of the West Valley site because of its location between two known northeast–southwest trending fault systems. One of these is the "Bass Island Trend," extending northeast from Chautauqua Lake. It is shallow and considered inactive, but possibly overlaying an older, deeper, active fault. The other is a branch of the ancient and active Clarendon-Linden Fault, called the "Attica Splay," that points southwestward from Batavia directly at the West Valley site. Combined with evidence of folds and fractures in the gorge wall and the rapid and surprisingly straight cut of the Zoar Valley, this pattern suggests that the area has been seismically active and could be still—not a welcome prospect given the 10,000-year radioactive life of some of the buried wastes. Oral history further suggests active faults, as in this note from Eber Russell: "As early as 1825 the settlers were telling of the 'Terrible ravines and Breakers of the Cattaraugus Creek.' The cliffs are continually breaking away, sometimes in a thundering rock fall or 'break.' There is a cave (Indian) the result of an earthquake fault."[9]

I volunteered my help in the coalition's faultfinding mission in exchange for Ray's help in finding the wizard's cave. We picked up Colleen, another coalition member, and headed to a hill just north of West Valley where they had been taking measurements on a section of the Canadaway shale exposed by a downcutting brook. Near the base of the hill at the first erosion-resistant ledge, Ray took out his equipment: a tape measure, an "inclinometer" (a homemade sort of dial with a level on the back and 360 degree marks around the circumference), a compass, and a length of garden hose, transparent at either end. I held one end of the tape measure to the top edge of the ledge while Colleen took the other and walked to the next prominent ledge, about 50 feet up the brook. Ray used his dial to get the angle between. With these two measurements and a topographic map, he could calculate the vertical rise between strata and their relative location within the Canadaway Formation.

In this way we proceeded upstream, from ledge to ledge, until we reached a distinctive 3-inch thick shelf of siltstone, nicknamed "the Madonna layer" by the coalition. Here Ray filled the garden hose with water, aligning the water level at one end with the top of the outcrop in the creek bed. Colleen held the hose's other end near an outcrop of the Madonna about 40 feet downstream, until the water reached the same height as Ray's. Since water seeks its own level, the distance between the top of Colleen's water and the top of her section of the Madonna gave a measurement of the strata's apparent dip and strike (directional orientation). With hundreds of other measurements like these, and using the least squares method (kids, just get out your geometry books) to plot the approximate plane in which they fall, the coalition has begun to fill out the picture on fault and fracture networks within the area's bedrock strata.[10]

Erosion is the other major threat for all downstream from the West Valley site. Radioactive wastes are buried in trenches dug into glacial clays overlying the bedrock and adjacent to steep ravines. As erosion widens and deepens these ravines, they will cut into the trenches, allowing radioactive material to spill into the fast-flowing tributaries of Cattaraugus Creek. In their consideration of future options for securing the site, the DOE draft environmental impact statements acknowledge that high-level radioactive contamination downstream is a possible future consequence of uncontrolled erosion.

For the coalition, the only safe solution to the problem at West Valley is to dig up the waste and contain it above ground where it can be monitored safely until a suitably stable long-term storage environment can be found. In the short term, this is by far the most expensive option. So the coalition also wants "full cost accounting" for *all* proposed clean-up scenarios, including the government's early preferred option of containing the buried waste in place. Containment may sound cheaper, they say, but this is a water-dominated landscape whose streams keep carving away at the solid ground. How much will containment cost over the next 10,000 years?—assuming Good Mind prevails that long to continue the task.

THE WIZARD OF GUSTANGO

THE "MAP OF HODENOSAUNEEGA," you may remember, says *Oat-gont* is "the wizard of Gustango" and "Gustango," says Eber Russell, is the name of an old Indian village now occupied by the village of Versailles, just across a bridge from Seneca Nation land. Citing Arthur Parker's research, Russell describes Gustango/Versailles as one of twenty known prehistoric village sites in the Cattaraugus Valley representing at least four distinct cultural occupations. These reach back in time to just after the Ice Age (Russell collected a mastodon effigy pipe near Versailles), to a later series of sites related by their pottery fragments, to a mound or two representing an intrusion of the Ohio Valley-based mound builders, to a number of sites characterized by earth rings— remnants of the walled and sometimes double-walled villages of the Erie Nation, said to have been vanquished or absorbed by the Senecas in the mid-1600s.

Versailles should have been included in the Cattaraugus Reservation, but was not due to the trickery and deceit of the Holland Land Company. "When the surveyors approached what is now the hamlet of Versailles they discovered that if the line were turned West at the agreed point it would leave an excellent water power site on Indian land. So the line ran ½ mile further North before turning West."[11] In the 1860s and 1870s, Versailles Botanic Mills ground and mixed medicines from local barks, roots, and herbs using "ancient Indian recipes."

Ray and I went to the only place there is for a stranger to go in Versailles, Sprague's General Store—a down-home emporium with two wooden aisles stocked with beer, candy bars, fishing tackle, machine parts, videos, and the owner's personal collection of stones and hunting memorabilia, including an autographed print of a twelve-point buck wishing him better luck next year. We asked Gary, the proprietor, who asked John, a customer, who referred us to his dad who lived down the road and whose front gate bore a sign "Arthritis Acres. We've got a crick in the back." None of them had heard of the Wizard of Gustango, the naked hero, or the cave.

As we continued to explore the Zoar Valley gorge looking for caves and fault lines, we began to notice, in measures that increased with time spent on the creek, the great stands of cedar and hemlock; the families of kingfishers and cliff swallows, turkey vultures and eagles; the play of translucent green light on creekbed shale; the particular magic and power of the place itself. On one feeder stream, where the cut banks were seeping oil and the creek itself bubbling like a pot of boiling water, we put a match to a bubble and, *poof*, a column of flame shot up. We performed this wizardly trick a few more times, gratified with a torch from every bubble.

6.4. LIGHTING THE CREEK. PHOTO COURTESY
OF KATHY MCGOLDRICK.

NAKED TRUTH IS A DEEP DISGUISE

A YEAR OR TWO after finding the map, I attended a slide lecture on the Zoar Valley presented by local historian Phil Palen at the Gowanda Historical Society. The essence of Phil's talk was that no one has ever managed to tame this wilderness. He clicked through two hundred images of the various attempts. Here were Lloyd and Evelyn Valentine and their five children who began farming the flats in 1925 and gave it up in 1945; here the hippie encampments of the 1960s; here the tombstone of one of the many who have drowned or fallen in the gorge; here the old glue factory now a languishing Superfund site.

And then, two photos of "the Indian Cave": one taken from Lookout Point; the second from inside the cave—an 80-foot deep fissure, according to Phil—looking out through its narrow mouth over the valley. The *otgont* perspective, you might say.

Phil did not say who took this photo.

SINCE PHIL SOLVED THE MYSTERY, I have been back to Lookout Point many times to contemplate the meaning of that dark spot on the north canyon wall and the two fragments of cultural genesis myths that intersect here.

In the Haudenosaunee creation story, it seems that the cave serves to remind us of our limited understanding of the order of things, but also of Good Mind's imminence in all creation. The biblical story of Zoar, on the other hand, suggests that nature, including human nature, is largely "wicked" and therefore rightfully destroyed except for a small saved remnant of right-minded people.

Seneca scholar John Mohawk reflects on the implications of these contrasting cosmologies: "The idea that human beings have an imperfect understanding of the rational nature of existence is something of a caution to Haudenosaunee in their dealing with nature. Conversely, the idea that the natural world is disorganized and irrational has served as something of a permission in the West and may be the single cultural aspect which best explains the differences between these two societies' relationships to Nature."[12]

In Western cosmology, as Mohawk labels it, it's a fairly straight line from Ahaz Allen's Zoar to my generation's permission to store and then leave radioactive waste buried at West Valley. Apparently rational proce-dures like the environmental impact assessment can conceal a deep gulf between our limited understanding of the natural world and our unlimited ability to inflict lasting damages.

Or, to give the last word to Eber Russell with an assist from Wendell Berry, "Naked truth (the relative smallness of our knowledge) is a deep disguise which those accustomed to deceive cannot often penetrate."

INTERLUDE

Killdeer and Other Mysteries

JULY 19, 1991. Wading along an open beachy stretch of Cattaraugus Creek, we flush, from apparently nowhere, a long-legged brown bird and its young. Four fledglings, all grey and dun-brown, are almost invisible against the muds and sands of the creekbed except for the black rings round their necks, which semicircle around to the back of us, like the floating grins of four Cheshire cats. The killdeer parent flies to a point a few yards ahead, commanding our attention when she lands by raising two orange flags on the undersides of her wings. She is the majorette; we the parade. She hobbles upstream in front of us, dragging her wing in the water, rolling, lolling, staggering, sometimes going belly-up, all the time shrieking while we follow, as we are supposed to, transfixed by the performance. When we are safely enough past the young ones, she flies off, quite professionally, and joins them downstream.

We splash on, picking up small flat rocks as we go and carefully replacing them. Under nearly every one is a little clown-striped, pointy-nosed fish: young sticklebacks. Also crayfish, waterpennies, water beetles, and dragonfly larvae—fat and segmented little monsters without their wings. Cliff swallows swoop in and out of cracks in the gorge wall, which bends with the creek to the right. In this elbow we find some odd footprints—two spiraling grooves etched deep into the sediments, each one maybe 6 feet across.

"What the heck is that?" says my eleven-year-old son.

We discuss the possibilities of alien spacecraft landing gear while gazing at the flowing water bouncing off the north canyon wall. We decide that maybe, after last week's heavy rain, the current was forceful enough to cut these whirlpool patterns into the mud before spinning off into the next meander.

No sooner have we solved this mystery than the creek presents us with another. Here, on the switchback trail back out of the gorge, are dozens of tan, golf-ball-sized, papery-skinned spheres on the ground under the sugar maples, some with bits of stem and leaf attached. Inside these balls lies the mystery. It's mostly air, surrounding a small brown "seed" fixed in the center by a symmetrically radiating structure of spikes connecting to the inner wall of the outer sphere. Every single paper ball has a little hole in both its outer shell and in the "seed" inside. We figure it is some kind of maple ball gall, like those we've seen on goldenrod stems and know to be made by a plant hormone to imprison the voracious larvae of the tiny peacock fly, so named for its elaborate wing-fanning displays.

But why this intricate structure? Has an insect somehow caused the manufacture of these delicate balls within balls to protect its grub, perhaps to float if it falls in water? Or does the double envelope and air pocket somehow protect the maple better than a simple crust would do? Or is it those trickster aliens again, confounding us with their false clues and otgont inventions.

PART III

THE EASTERN DOOR

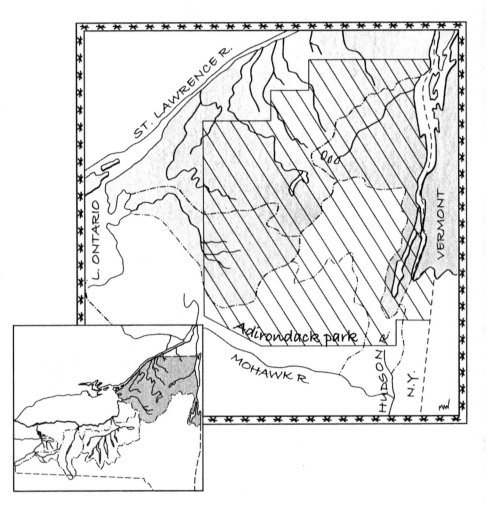

7.1 ADIRONDACK WATERSHEDS TRIBUTARY TO LAKE ONTARIO
AND THE ST. LAWRENCE RIVER

SEVEN

HIGH PEAKS, CLOUD LAKES

"Does smoke talk with the clouds?"
—Pablo Neruda,
The Book of Questions

FLATLANDERS LIVING IN THE Great Lakes-Midwest regions may recognize their links with the Adirondack Mountains even less than North Country people think of their ties to the sweetwater seas. But the connections are there.

The Adirondack Park is the largest public park in the contiguous United States. Since 1894, close to half of its six million acres have been protected as "forever wild" by the New York State Constitution. Mountain ranges within those six million acres define five major drainage basins, three of them tributary to the lower Great Lakes and their outlet to the Atlantic Ocean. Streams flowing off the central highlands feed Lake Ontario via the Black River to the west, the St. Lawrence River to the north, Lake Champlain to the east, and the Hudson and Mohawk rivers to the south.

Over three thousand lakes and ponds and tens of thousands of miles of brooks and streams delicately point the rough-hewn Adirondack landscape with its mile-high mountains rooted 9 miles deep into the earth's crust. The whole seems to be in a relatively dynamic state of balance. Mountains succumbing to the slow process of water and wind erosion also are rising or "doming" (a localized uplift whose precise

7.2. ADIRONDACK HIGHLANDS

agent remains unclear) at a rate of 3 millimeters per year.[1] Forests expand and contract as resource extraction industries, real estate developers, and preservationists contend within the Blue Line. Native species come and go through naturally occurring and human-caused reintroductions, and in response to changes in habitat and water quality that originate, in some cases, far beyond the boundaries of the park.

In terms of the Great Lakes hydrologic cycle, the Adirondack cloudlands, though the birthplace of tributary rivers, are very much at the downstream end. This is a complicated story and as various as its different tellers, but I will try to sort out some of it here.

EVERY SUMMER for the past twenty-five years I have gone to the Adirondacks for a dose of their "forever wild" and returned to the lake plains full of story material for my friends and family—stories about encounters with bears or with weird Adirondack hermits living in state camping grounds with pet cats and memories of how things were before the Northway sped folks right through from Albany to Montréal. As a "forty-sixer," I share a whole category of stories with other pilgrims who have climbed the forty-six peaks over 4,000 feet. The

mere word "Couchsacraga" bonds us in memory of bodily mortifica-
tion along an endless trail-less trek to a blasted viewless peak. Adirondack animals have generously appeared and magically disappeared
before me—black bear, coyote, whitetail deer, otter, beaver, osprey, loon,
raven, muskrat, mink—I can conjure each one in the specific woods or
pool where we met.

But over the years, and for however much I need to believe in this
place of always wild, it has become harder not to notice that all is not
well in the Adirondacks.

The giveaway is the fish.

I have never eaten an Adirondack fish, or had an opportunity to.
This never struck me as strange until about ten years ago when I was
hiking into the Siamese Ponds Wilderness Area and met a fisherman
walking the same trail following the east branch of the Sacandaga
River. I asked him about the fishing and he explained that it was no
good back at the lake where he had just been and where I was camping. He said that the state Department of Environmental Conservation
had treated the lake with rotenone, a poison that kills off most gill-
breathing aquatic life, in order to reintroduce the highly prized native
brook trout that have died out in most Adirondack lakes. Rotenone is
used in some of the smaller lakes to kill the competition, especially
introduced species like yellow perch and bass. However, it takes some
time for a lake to recover from such a general poisoning and for the
stocked trout to take hold. This angler was hiking into the wilderness
area to find fish in untreated waters. He did not seem that hopeful.

For a long time after that I thought the reason I never saw an angler
catch anything on my lake—we'll call it "Barkeater," said to be the
meaning of "Adirondack," a term the Iroquois scornfully applied to their
Algonquin enemies—was the lingering effects of rotenone applications.

Then I began observing one of the ponds that feeds Barkeater
Lake. This pond lies in a depression near the top of a small mountain at
about 2,200 feet above sea level. It is a typical higher elevation pond
whose waters depend mainly on clouds that snag on the ragged peak.
In the early 1900s, the mountain's heart of industrial-grade garnet was
discovered (garnets are still mined hereabouts for use as industrial abra-
sives), and the pond's outlet was dammed so its water could be used for
processing. When the mine played out in the late 1920s, the company

abandoned it, leaving a raw crater where the mountaintop had been, along with tailing mounds, dynamite shacks, dam, and a mile or so of pipeline. Eventually the dam was partially breached, affording the pond a trickle of drainage through its old brook outlet down to the lake.

Here let us digress for a moment to remember that the entire Adirondack "wilderness" was once logged and mined almost into oblivion. Abandoned mines have left many visible and who knows what invisible scars there. Until relatively recent mine closure laws forced long-delayed restorations, mining industries appear to have simply walked away from big operations like the Tahawus ironworks in the central Adirondacks, or the series of garnet mines around Barkeater Lake. John Huston's film, *The Treasure of the Sierra Madre* (1948), directly addresses such practice when the old man Howard (played by Walter Huston) lectures the greedy Dobbs (Humphrey Bogart) on the need to put back the mountain they have just mined of its gold. "We have wounded this mountain and I think it is our duty to close its wounds," says Walter Huston at his cantankerous best. "The silent beauty of this place deserves our respect. Besides, I want to think of this place the way we found it and not as it has been while we were taking away its treasures, which this same mountain has guarded for millions of years. I couldn't sleep well thinking I had left the mountain looking like a junkyard. I'm sorry we can't do this restoration perfectly—that we can do no better than show our good intention and gratitude."[2]

THE THING ABOUT my Adirondack pond is that it, like Barkeater Lake, seemed to contain no fish, though I am quite sure it was never treated with rotenone. Its still black waters were home to great numbers of a fairly limited number of species: adult newts, dragonflies, damselflies, and the smaller insects they feed on. But never, over the course of some twenty Augusts, did I see a fish, bird, or mammal there. Representing the plant kingdom was a submerged forest of tree stumps, probably from when the pond was dammed, and a groundcover of round-leaved sundews dominating the open edge between the water and surrounding woods of balsam, hemlock, and spruce. On the earth embankment at the dammed end of the pond I found one year a bed of miniature stemmed plants full of red pods the size of a swollen grain of rice. Curious, I slit open a bulging little pod with my thumbnail and found inside a tiny twirling red worm. I opened a dozen more. Every one held such a spinner. So add this, whatever its is, predator or prey, to the pond food web.

This community suggests that the pond was on its way to becoming a bog, another quite natural phenomenon in the Adirondacks where lack of inflow and outflow leads to poor aeration. Lower oxygen levels mean there will be fewer bacteria to decompose plants. As dead plant materials accumulate, they acidify the water, and as acidity increases, living plants become less able to absorb nutrients through their root hairs. Most species will die out. But a few plants with special adaptations, like the carnivorous sundews with their sticky tentacles for trapping and digesting insects, will thrive.

Fish require at least somewhat oxygenated, pH-neutral water to live and reproduce. According to New York State's surface water quality standards, most fish need at least 5 milligrams of dissolved oxygen per liter of water; trout need a minimum of 6, and spawning trout at least 7. On the pH scale of 0 to 14—with 0 extremely acid, 14 extremely alkaline, and 7 neutral—Adirondack waterbodies with a pH below 6 are rated "endangered" in terms of their ability to support fish, and "critical" if the pH is below 5.[3] (Each number going up the pH scale multiplies acidity by a factor of 10.)

Perhaps some species of amphibians are more adaptable. Amphibians, after all, can come to the surface to breathe, and they live parts of their lives completely outside the water. Spotted newts seem able to survive the harshest conditions of all. They were clearly top predators in this pond, while their youth, the stalwart but delicate red efts, could often be found hiking, by millimeters, the mountain trails and even the rocky summits where they stick out like sore thumbs.

I concluded that high acidity might be part of the reason why there were no fish in the pond and began wondering whether acid rain might be a contributing factor here or in other apparently fishless Adirondack lakes.

In August 1997, on my way up Whiteface Mountain, the most northern and fifth highest Adirondack peak at 4,867 feet, I detoured briefly into the Atmospheric Sciences Research Center to talk with a scientist who was reading computer printouts of data from the air sampling equipment there. His response to my questions was definitive:

"Acid rain is no longer a problem up here—hasn't been for ten years. People are still stuck on old data."

A few days later I carried this news to Ray Fadden, or Tehanetorens to use his Mohawk name, who founded the Six Nations Museum in Onchiota in 1954 and who has lived in the northern Adirondacks for almost a century. Tehanetorens is a master storyteller with a tart sense of humor, but on this occasion he became angry. He said that the fish in the ponds and streams around him were dying and that even the plants were showing signs of poisoning. He was feeding the wildlife, including eleven bears, to help them survive the loss of natural food sources and viable habitat.[4]

In 2003, I ventured into the DEC regional headquarters in Ray Brook where a display said that 24 percent, or 346 of the 1,469 once fishable lakes they surveyed in the Adirondacks, now had no fish life. At least twenty of the largest lakes, including Lake Champlain, were polluted with mercury, a potent neurotoxin so lethal that one-eighth of a teaspoon can contaminate a 20-acre lake. For children and women of childbearing age, fish from these lakes were not safe to eat. The New York State attorney general had filed suits against coal-fired electric utilities in Ohio and several other midwestern states, as well as in upstate New York as the major releasers of the sulfur dioxide (SO2), nitrous oxide (NOx) and mercury that are poisoning forests, lakes, and rivers in the Adirondacks. His office was also seeking intervention through the Commission on Environmental Cooperation, a cross-border environmental dispute resolution sidearm to the North American Free Trade Agreement, to make the province of Ontario enforce its laws, on the grounds that power plants in southern Ontario are the source of at least 20 percent of the sulfur deposition in the Adirondacks.[5]

Wow. How did I not know this? Equipped with a little pump water filter, I hike, camp, and drink these mountains, assuming the higher I go, the healthier the air and water. It's hard to grasp that Whiteface Mountain is out of compliance with national air quality standards, or that alpine ponds and lakes could be dying from pollutant-laden rain, fog, and snow blown in from the flatlands to the west.

7.3. "The STS-92 Space Shuttle Astronauts photographed upstate New York at sunset on October 21, 2000. Water bodies (Lake Ontario, Lake Erie, the Finger Lakes, the St. Lawrence, and the Niagara rivers) are highlighted by sunlight. The photograph captures a regional smog layer extending across central New York. The layer of pollution is capped by an atmospheric inversion, which is marked by the layer of clouds at the top." Image and caption courtesy of the Image Science + Analysis Laboratory, NASA Johnson Space Center.

EXPERT TESTIMONY

AS IT TURNS OUT, people who live in the Adirondacks have written volumes on acid rain based on several decades' worth of firsthand experience with its effects on their local ecosystems and economies. In his book, *Acid Rain, Acid Snow,* poet-activist John Slade describes the changes he has witnessed under the water of an Adirondack lake.

> I have snorkeled in my beloved Adirondack Lake every summer for forty-three years . . . In 1959, while snorkling for an hour, I would see hundreds of fish, especially in the lilypad jungles. Snails and snail eggs were on nearly every sunken stick. The swarms of daphnia were so thick, like clouds of dancing fairy motes, it seemed as if the small fish would never run out of an abundant dinner. Forty years later, in 1999 . . . most of the animal life had vanished.[6]

Anne LaBastille, author of scientific articles on wildlife ecology and popular books documenting her own experience living in the Adirondack wilderness, published "Death From the Sky" in 1988.[7] She noticed the disappearance of the most visible aquatic life in her lake, Black Bear Lake, in the 1970s. She began taking pH readings of the lake and surrounding ponds and compared them to what historical data she could find. In 1933, the pH of Black Bear Lake measured 6.3. In 1983, her readings were between 4.1 and 4.5, meaning that the lake had become about one hundred times more acidic in fifty years.

Her research took her to Norway and Sweden, countries hard hit by acidic deposition from sources as far away as Great Britain and northern Europe. At a UN meeting on long-range air transport of air pollution she heard expert testimony from Scandinavian delegates appealing to upwind countries to stop the pollution, and other expert testimony from England and Germany saying there was no scientific evidence linking the smoke from their power plants and factories to the demise of fish and forests in Scandinavia. Eventually *Waldsterban,* or "forest death," took over 50 percent of West Germany's mountain firs, pines, spruces and beeches, causing Germany to reverse its position on acid rain and adopt stringent air pollution controls for power plants, vehicles, and factories.

In 2005, the Adirondack Council testified before the Senate Environment and Public Works Committee against President George W. Bush's deceptively titled "Clear Skies Act of 2005" and for stronger federal legislation to address the problem of acid rain:

> The Adirondack Park has suffered some of the greatest damage from acid rain due to its geology and geography . . . On many mountaintops, 80 percent of the lush red spruce and balsam fir forests have turned brown and died as the soil has been poisoned. Sugar maples and the maple industry are also profoundly affected by acid rain. Acid rain has reduced the pH of some of our lakes to the same level as vinegar . . . New York has now taken exhaustive measures to clean up its own plants. We are now asking the rest of the country to do the same.[8]

THINK LOCALLY, ACT GLOBALLY

"NORTH CREEK supports Gore Mountain wind" reads the shop window signs in my own adopted Adirondack village. The proposal is to put up a wind farm on neighboring Gore Mountain at an abandoned garnet mine site ideally suited for the purpose in terms of past development, existing infrastructure, and prevailing winds. Long-time residents generally support it as a way to expand the local economy and job base for the next generation. But many newer property owners— people who have recently purchased a piece of the Adirondack dream—don't want things to change, including their mountain view.

In fact, Adirondack communities are well situated to develop low-impact green energy sources like wind not only because they get lots of it, but also because many of them, due to their remoteness, already are equipped with decentralized power. This I learned firsthand on August 14, 2003, when the laundromat in Saranac Lake where I was doing my wash suddenly went dark along with the rest of the northeastern United States and Canada. What to do? My entire wardrobe was in "soak." Someone mentioned that they thought Long Lake might have power, so I hauled my soggy clothes 30 miles down the road and, sure enough, Long Lake's machines were up and running. Long Lake and a few other villages simply switched over to their local generator and never lost power.

However, like global warming, acid rain is one of those "tragedy of the commons" problems that cannot be addressed through local action alone. It requires state, federal, and ultimately global regulation, for which there are profound disincentives, not least the idea that there is a competitive advantage to the industry, state, or country that does not have to invest in emission controls. Moreover, the time and distances involved between smokestacks and dead lakes make it hard to pinpoint the culprits, and there are plenty of attorneys able to muster expert testimony on behalf of their corporate clients.

After the 1970 Clean Air Act was passed, many coal-fired power plants met new regional standards for cleaner air by building taller smokestacks, up to 1,000 feet tall, and downwind high-altitude regions were hit even harder than before. The 1990 amendments to the Clean Air Act mandated further reductions of industrial releases of sulfur dioxide and nitrous oxide (40 percent and 10 percent, respectively) and set a national cap for sulfur dioxide emissions of 15.4 million tons annually to be achieved by 2010, though they set no cap on nitrous oxide emissions, and no standards or caps for mercury releases from power plants.

As a result of a monitoring network in the Northeast, we now know that forest and lake recovery will require much deeper cuts in fossil fuel emissions. For example, acid deposition destroys the buffering capacity of soils by destroying base elements like calcium and magnesium, making them more vulnerable over the long term. It also leaches aluminum into soil and waters, and high aluminum concentrations are directly toxic to fish. Adirondack lakes with no fish have consistently lower pH, lower acid-neutralizing capacity, and higher aluminum concentrations than lakes with one or more fish species. The Hubbard Brook Research Foundation and the U. S. Forest Service, who have been monitoring and modeling acid rain deposition in the Northeast since the early 1960s, summarize these findings:

> Acid deposition . . . has had greater impact on soils, surface waters, and trees than previously projected. Although the 1970 and 1990 Clean Air Acts have had positive effects, emis-

sions remain high compared to background conditions. Given the accumulation of acids and loss of buffering capacity in the soil, many areas in the Northeast are now more sensitive to acid deposition and have developed an inertia that will delay recovery.[9]

According to their models, an additional 80 percent reduction in electric utility sulfur dioxide emissions would enable Adirondack streams and soils to approach recovery thresholds by 2050, assuming all else remained equal. However, unless caps are set for the other pollutants from coal-burning power plants, all else will not remain equal, and even an 80 percent reduction in SO2 releases will not be enough to restore healthy fish to Adirondack waters.

A SECOND CHANCE

IN *The End of Nature*, Adirondack writer Bill McKibben explores another impact of fossil fuel burning—the buildup of carbon dioxide in the earth's atmosphere and consequent climate destabilization. A few years after publishing this depressing book, McKibben wrote a sort of antidote, *Hope, Human and Wild*, based largely on his experience of the Adirondacks. Here, as he puts it, the forest has retained "sufficient vigor to reassert itself—for its original species to press up through the weight of our settlement and reestablish themselves." The Adirondacks have given us "a second chance," he says, and, notwithstanding the global problems of acid rain and climate change, I cannot help agreeing. But just what does this second chance consist of? What elements are at work on behalf of life beneath the human footprint?

BARKEATER LAKE, the stand of water I know best in the Adirondacks, is a smallish north–south oriented lake, about 2 miles long and a quarter-mile wide, at an elevation of 1,700 feet. Its north end has a public campground and launch for nonmotorized boats; its south end backs into a 50-square-mile forest broken only by a few foot trails. At this southern end, the lake gradually transforms into a marsh of rushes, waterlily, arrowhead, and pickerelweed. However, if you look carefully, you can find a clear channel of flowing water leading to a beaver dam holding up a pond and, in the middle of the pond, a lodge that has been there for so long it has itself become an island of living shrubs and trees.

All life on the lake, along with the prevailing wind and water currents, seems to originate in this beaver labyrinth. Canoeing down to it, we find, with every passing year, another outlying lodge belonging to a new family of beaver, each located at the mouth of a small freshet entering the lake's east side. (On the west side, the mountains drop steeply into the water, leaving no such habitat-friendly marshy edge.) We often see a big group of common mergansers, an adult or two with as many as a dozen juveniles, browsing or practicing their paddle wheeling along the coves close to shore. Within a half-mile of the beaver labyrinth, the many ears and eyes of its entrance marsh always announce our approach. Swallows and cedar waxwings dart out to our canoe, then back to the great white pines on high points of land thrust into the lake. A pair of osprey alert each other with their eagle whistles, the loons tremolo and dive, the shape-shifting great blue heron finally gives up looking like a snag and flaps off further south into the heart of beaver country.

One August morning my husband Neil and I portaged our canoe over the entrance dam and followed a winding corridor of ponds and grassy narrows for several miles through a landscape completely shaped by beaver. Seven dams raised the most interior water levels a full 6 feet above the lake. Feeding platforms of floating aspen branches had become islands. The waterway was beaver width, and the white, dog-turdish scats clearly visible on the bottom seemed to be supporting a healthy population of crayfish dining on them. An adult merganser resting on a rock ahead hissed as we approached and clumsily swam away as we backpaddled. It was the same one we'd noticed at the north end of the lake the day before, rolling and high-stepping on a dock, trying to free itself from 2 feet of fishing line and lures tangled around its legs. It had found its way to this sanctuary to either free itself or die.

Beaver were trapped out of the Adirondacks long ago, with only one known active colony remaining in all of New York State in the early 1900s. The state released six beaver in the Adirondacks in 1904 and twenty-five more in 1906, and now New York's beaver population numbers well over 100,000. They have returned and prospered, so much so that they have designed much of the park as we know it, from the thousands of small ponds to the marshes, swamps, and wet meadows found near even the highest mountain summits.

As we discovered last summer, beaver have taken over the boggy pond that feeds Barkeater Lake, and transformed it. At the outlet where the garnet mine dam had been built and then breached, the beaver have constructed their own dam—a long, sinuous, buttressed affair that snakes across the entire lower end, raising the pond's water level by a foot or more. For the first time in twenty years, we saw fish and birds in the pond: minnows, mallards, heron, blue-winged teal. Reeds, arrowhead, wild iris, and other flowering plants are growing in the shallows, where the sundews used to be. Across the way, we saw the sparkling wakes of two small animals bobbing in and out of the water. Otter? Beaver kits? The whole pond looked alive. I finally remembered to bring a pH test kit, which gave readings of 6.5 to 7.0—close to neutral. Whether the high water diluted acidity or simply created better year-round conditions for fish and other aquatic life, pond life seems to have benefited.

In her book, *Water: A Natural History*, Alice Outwater describes beaver as "nature's hydrologists," whose decline "caused the first major shift in the country's water cycle."

> It is estimated that as many as two hundred million beavers once lived in the continental United States, their dams making meadows out of forests, their wetlands slowly capturing silt. The result of the beaver's engineering was a remarkably uniform buildup of organic material in the valleys, a checkerboard of meadows through the woodlands, and a great deal of edge, that fruitful zone where natural communities meet. Beavers are a keystone species, for where beavers build dams, the wetlands spread out behind them, providing home and food for dozens of species, from migrating ducks to moose, from fish to frogs to great blue herons.[10]

Not to mention people. New York City owes its excellent water supply in part to the chains of reservoirs built by beaver, beginning with Lake Tear of the Clouds at the source of the Hudson River. Thus,

7.4. BEAVER DAM AT LAKE TEAR OF THE CLOUDS.
COURTESY MAUREEN WALL.

if the Adirondacks have provided a second chance at restoring and
maintaining a healthy ecosystem, it has not been entirely up to us. In
fact, we had virtually destroyed the forest ecosystem by the end of the
nineteenth century through unsustainable logging, forest fires, resource
extraction (including decimation of the fur-bearing animal populations), and, consequent to all of these pressures, siltation, pollution, and
degradation of its waters. True, the main ingredient for recovery was the
recognition by advocates, and finally the state legislature, of the value of
the region as a water supply for New York City. Because of this, an
1894 amendment to the state constitution ensures that state holdings
within the park cannot "be leased, sold or exchanged . . . nor shall the
timber thereon be sold, removed or destroyed."

But with these protections in place, other agents for recovery came
into play. The beaver, for example, have so reworked the landscape by
retaining the water that locally extirpated species like the otter and
moose have come back on their own.

The Adirondack "forever wild" experiment has taught us much. We
have learned on the one hand that the task of restoring a watershed is

much larger than we thought—that it requires, for example, national energy policies that reduce or eliminate discharges of long-lived pollutants that wind up in lakes and streams. On the other hand we have also learned that it is not all entirely up to us. Our second chance resides in recognizing the importance of other species that have coevolved with their native places, and ensuring that we leave them the resources they need to help bring those ecosystems back.

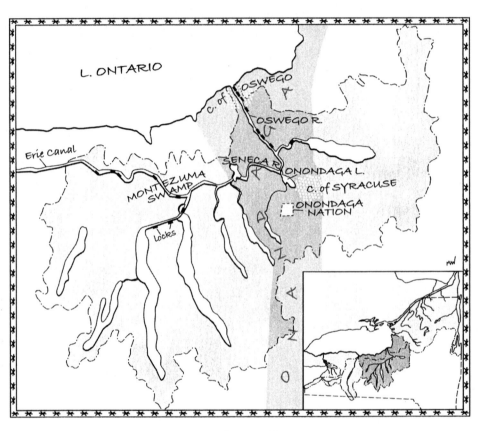

8.1 Oswego River Watershed

EIGHT

OSWEGO, ONONDAGA, AND THE POLITICS OF LISTING

> The Onondaga people wish to bring about a healing
> between themselves and all others who live in this region
> that has been the homeland of the Onondaga Nation since
> the dawn of time. The Nation and its people have a unique
> spiritual, cultural, and historic relationship with the land,
> which is embodied in *Gayanashagowa*, the Great Law of
> Peace. This relationship goes far beyond federal and state
> legal concepts of ownership, possession, or other legal rights.
> The people are one with the land and consider themselves
> stewards of it. It is the duty of the Nation's leaders to work
> for a healing of this land, to protect it, and to pass it on to
> future generations. The Onondaga Nation brings this action
> on behalf of its people in the hope that it may hasten the
> process of reconciliation and bring lasting justice, peace, and
> respect among all who inhabit this area.
>
> —*The Onondaga Nation v. the State of New York et al.*,
> March 11, 2005

WE TURN NOW to the Oswego River with respect for the vastness of its
watershed, the range of fish and wildlife migrations it has enabled, and
the sacred Superfund lake that feeds it.

"Oswego" [osh-we-geh] by most accounts means "pouring out
place." Formed by the confluence of the Oneida and the Seneca rivers,

8.2. LOCK ON THE OSWEGO RIVER

the Oswego River drains 5,000 square miles of central New York—
"the Three Rivers Watershed." It is second only to the Niagara as a
major tributary to Lake Ontario. The Seneca River branch is by far the
largest contributor, collecting waters from Onondaga Lake, the Finger
Lakes, and Montezuma Swamp, which spans central New York north of
the Fingers like the hollow palm of an open hand.

A fort near the river's mouth, in what is now the city of Oswego,
dates back to 1622, attesting to the strategic importance of what would
become the Great Lakes' easternmost American port. Fort Oswego
"saw action in every major war of this country," the guide there will tell
you—from the French and Indian Wars to World War II, when it served
as a refugee camp for Holocaust survivors. The river cuts wide and fast
through the middle of the city. If you follow it upstream from the little
vestigial port at its mouth, you will distinguish three rivers in one channel: a middle current galloping boisterously down its final stretch to
Lake Ontario, and two side streams slightly higher and tamer, backed up

behind locks or hydropower dams. On the east side, four locks step boats down the Oswego River's final drop to the great lake; on the west bank, three hydropower dams capture the river's flow.

MIGRATIONS

HISTORICALLY, the Oswego-Three Rivers watershed accommodated some of the most astounding animal migrations on the planet, including the spawning and maturation cycles of the Atlantic salmon and the American eel. Two of the long-term restoration goals for the Oswego River, at least for the Lower Great Lakes office of the U.S. Fish and Wildlife Service, are to bring these species back.

No one knows exactly why diadromous (literally, "running between") fish travel between salt and freshwater to reproduce, some investing years swimming thousands of miles up or downstream, eventually retracing their way all the way back to their natal spawning grounds. The catadromous ("running down") American eel, a fish that lives most of its life in freshwater and breeds at sea, once accounted for up to half the aquatic biomass in the region tributary to the St. Lawrence River and Lake Ontario, all the way in to the first impassable barrier: Niagara Falls.[1] "A man could spear a thousand in one night," wrote a Jesuit diarist of the Oswego eel run in the 1780s. As recently as 1995, the American eel was the third most valuable species in Canada's Lake Ontario and upper St. Lawrence River commercial fishery.[2]

American eels begin their lives as eggs hatching in the two-million-square-mile Sargasso Sea, a relatively warm, still, seaweed-rich lens of water created by a giant swirl of ocean currents southwest of Bermuda. Millions of larvae—each with the size, shape, and motor ability of a willow leaf—drift north in the Gulf Stream, some into the estuarine waters of the Gulf of St. Lawrence. In early spring, about a year after hatching, they metamorphose into miniature (2-inch) versions of their 3- to 5-foot-long adult eel bodies, capable of swimming but unpigmented at first (glass eels), gradually turning a greenish brown (elvers) in proximity to the land. Elvers slowly grow into juveniles (yellow eels) in freshwater, with the females spending the next three to twelve years migrating upstream, while the males linger in the estuary.

What we know about this migration we know mainly from a juvenile eel ladder installed in the Moses-Saunders Dam on the St. Lawrence River in 1974. Data collected there have shown that inland migration peaks in July and August and lasts about a month. Above the dam, the eels swim into Lake Ontario, up tributary rivers like the Oswego and on into headwaters like the Finger Lakes, where they may live another seven to thirty years as adults. They are carnivores (eating all manner of insects and aquatic animals, alive and dead) designed for travel, capable even of moving across wet grass and mud since they can absorb oxygen through their skin as well as their gills. Eventually, after reaching sexual maturity, the females metamorphose again to prepare for the three thousand-mile journey back to their spawning grounds. As silver eels, they store fat, cease feeding, lose excess baggage like their guts, swim back out to the estuary where the waiting males join them, and continue in pairs to the Sargasso Sea. Here the females release between twenty and forty million eggs apiece that the male partner fertilizes. After spawning, the adult eels die.

In 2006, the U.S. Fish and Wildlife Service held a series of research-sharing workshops around the country to consider whether to list the American eel as an endangered species. Listing a species is a sensitive subject. I know because they kicked me out of the New York meeting, though I had been invited by another invitee, Neil Patterson who, as a member of the Bear Clan and as Tuscarora director of the Haudenosaunee Environmental Task Force, has both a personal and professional interest in all fish of the lower Great Lakes. I left, but not before learning that, beginning with a mysterious major die-off in 1986, Great Lakes basin eel populations have declined to the point that there are no eels to be counted climbing the Moses-Saunders ladder, meaning virtually no migration into the upper St. Lawrence River and Lake Ontario.

The Great Lakes Fishery Commission posits three major reasons for this: the loss of upstream habitats from dams and other river modifications, mortalities of outmigrating females in power turbines (estimated at 25 to 40 percent), and harvesting of estuarine glass and elver eels, which fetch a high price on the Asian market.[3] The commission advocates reducing commercial fishing pressures in the estuary and mitigating the impacts of dams on migration. Complicating the obstacle course for eels is their own probable loss of capacity due to high

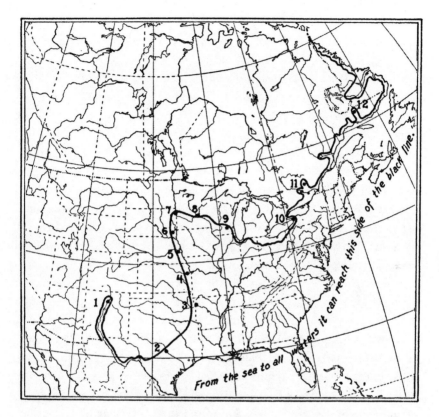

8.3. "NATIVE INLAND RANGE OF AMERICAN EEL: 10. NOT ABOVE NIAGARA FLALLS." MAP AND CAPTION FROM ERHARD ROSTLUND, *FRESHWATER FISH AND FISHING IN NATIVE NORTH AMERICA*, COURTESY UNIVERSITY OF CALIFORNIA PRESS.

burdens of contaminants like PCBs and mirex that have been found in the fat of estuarine eels. Females may be especially vulnerable, given their dependence on body fat in the grueling migration out to the Sargasso Sea.

Given this range of assaults and the rigorous scientific protocols for listing "endangered species"—rigorous because they may translate into regulations limiting corporate behavior—the American eel could go extinct before all the risks it faces can be sorted out and prioritized.

THE ANADROMOUS ("running up") Atlantic salmon migrate the opposite way. Salmon eggs hatch in shallow, cold headwater streams with
plenty of cover. The tiny fingerlings learn by doing, as Alice Outwater
describes in *Water: A Natural History.* They "survive dozens of predators,
and will hide, dart out, and zip back under cover to eat. They swim
alone. They know how to use rocks and logs to conserve energy, having
honed their swimming skills in variable, complex flows of a stream."[4]
Juveniles live in freshwater streams for two to three years before acquiring the armor of silver scales (smolt transformation) needed for migration. Adult Atlantic salmon once traveled out to sea where they lived
another few years, putting on weight, feeding in the great oceanic grazing grounds. When ready to spawn, females and males followed the St.
Lawrence River and other East Coast estuary rivers inland to their natal
streams, guided by remembered scent-marks.

Most Atlantic salmon in the St. Lawrence-Lake Ontario system
today are landlocked, spending their entire lives in freshwater, though
still migrating into tributary streams to spawn. What we know about
sea-run Atlantics in the Great Lakes is mainly from historical accounts.
In the Oswego River and Finger Lakes, they were so plentiful during
spawning that farmers reportedly used pitchforks to toss them on the
banks. (Note the overkill so often implied with these historical images
of abundance.) By 1898, few were found in Lake Ontario or its tributaries. Fish hatcheries continue to restock them but, as Outwater
observes, the very strengths that enabled young wild salmon to mature,
migrate, and spawn have so far defeated efforts to reintroduce hardy
stocks of reproducing fish. "Releasing hatchery fish to the wild may be
the piscine equivalent of sending a well-fed adolescent who has
watched a lot of television into the woods to survive on his wits."
Moreover, many of the conditions unfavorable to their survival persist,
including dams, low flows, pollution, and warmer waters.

Are there any remaining sea-run Atlantic salmon in the Oswego
River system? The answer depends on whom you ask. My Tuscarora
friend Neil, a dedicated fisherman, kindled my interest in the Oswego
River with this reply: "The proliferation of sea-run Atlantics throughout the Finger Lakes is not only true, it's amazing! Imagine how far
these fish were able to travel before dams on the Oswego." I understand
this to be the big picture on a long time horizon.

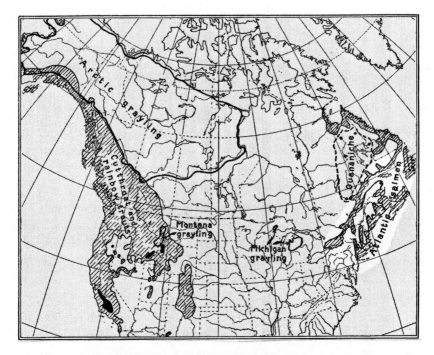

8.4. "NATIVE RANGE OF ATLANTIC SALMON." ROST-
LUND. COURTESY UNIVERSITY OF CALIFORNIA PRESS.

During the Moses-Saunders Dam relicensing negotiations, the New York Power Authority argued that sea-run salmon do not now and never have lived in the upper St. Lawrence or the Great Lakes; that the salmon historically found in Lake Ontario and its tributaries were landlocked salmon.[5] Biologists from the U.S. Geological Survey, the Bureau of Indian Affairs, and the Mohawk Nation disagreed, citing descriptions of salmon runs up the St. Lawrence dating back to the journals of Jacques Cartier and beyond in Mohawk oral history.

However, the power authority stuck to its story, and thereby eliminated the expense of providing for salmon passage at the dam. As Alice Outwater notes, "Although the salmon's life path was never easy, it has become unspeakably difficult to be anadromous today."

The EPA lists Atlantic salmon as an endangered species whose remaining wild range is restricted to the Gulf of Maine and its tributaries. The St. Regis Mohawk are experimenting with stocking fingerlings in

St. Lawrence tributaries, and the Onondaga Nation envisions bringing back the cold water Atlantic salmon fishery to a restored Onondaga Lake.

HISTORIC RUNS OF ATLANTIC SALMON and American eel into central New York via the Oswego River must have supported a rich interior biotic community, including the many species of birds stopping over and fueling up at Montezuma Swamp in spring and fall. The Montezuma National Wildlife Refuge and surrounding state-protected marshes and uplands, about 36,000 acres in all, are one of the Northeast's most important stopover areas for migratory birds.

Hundreds of thousands of waterfowl use the swamp, including Canada geese, snow geese, tundra swans, and dozens of species of ducks: mallard, gadwall, American wigeon, green-winged teal, canvasback, redhead, black, and scaup. Several species of heron along with Virginia rail, American bittern, sora, common moorhen, killdeer, spotted sandpiper, woodcock, and snipe breed on the territory. As does the bald eagle.

Bald eagles, the only species of eagle unique to North America, are long-lived (up to twenty-five years) top predators and mainly fish eaters. Thus, they were hit hard by contaminants accumulating in the lower Great Lakes food chain. Concentrations of DDT and other pesticides built up in their bodies over time, interfering with calcium levels and normal eggshell formation. Thin eggshells broke during incubation and the embryos died. The plight of the bald eagle helped spur the EPA to ban the use of DDT in 1972, and Congress to pass the Endangered Species Act in 1973.

New York's population was reduced to one pair in the western part of the state by the early 1970s. This stalwart pair nested in the same tree for over twenty years. During those decades, they were able to hatch and raise just one chick of their own. However, they became successful foster parents to many more captive-born chicks placed, literally, under their wing, and thus made a major contribution to the specie's rebound.

In 1976, the New York DEC began a hacking program to further these efforts at Montezuma Swamp. State biologists took immature bald eagles from wild nests in the upper Great Lakes, placed them in artificial nests on caged platforms atop high towers in remote areas of the swamp, and fed them until they could fly and hunt on their own. The state placed twenty-three eaglets at the refuge between 1976 and 1980 and attained the goal of twenty eagles successfully fledged. Through similar programs across the country, bald eagle populations increased to the point that in June 2007 the Interior Department removed them from the Endangered Species list. The EPA estimated over 10,000 mating pairs in the United States, mainly in Alaska, including 441 individuals in New York State, according to a 2006 winter count.

However, delisting the bald eagle was not simply a matter of reaching these goals. Property rights advocates pushed hard for it, including a Minnesota developer who sued the Interior Department for interfering with his right to develop 7 acres of land because of an eagle nest in the vicinity. Since bald eagles tend to return to and replenish their nests every year—old nests have been found up to 9 feet wide and 20 feet deep—listing under the Endangered Species Act protected nesting trees and buffer areas around them. Although bald eagles are still protected under other federal laws and treaties, nesting sites could be more at risk now that they are no longer listed as endangered.

THE OSWEGO RIVER AND THE ERIE CANAL

UP TO THIS POINT, we have not fully acknowledged that the Oswego-Three Rivers waterway is really more of a canal than a river system. The Oswego Canal, running 24 miles up the east side of the Oswego River was opened in 1828. It connects Lake Ontario to the Erie Canal system—524 miles of channelized rivers and manmade canal stretching across New York State from Lake Erie to the Hudson River, including spurs north to Lake Ontario and south to Cayuga Lake, the longest and deepest of the Finger Lakes.

As a commercial shipping route, the Erie Canal peaked in about 1880, after which it could not compete with the country's growing railroad system. In the early 1900s, New York built a canal three times larger and parallel to the original to accommodate commercial barges. However, the barge canal never fulfilled its economic promise, especially after the completion of the St. Lawrence Seaway and the interstate highway system. Barge traffic peaked in 1951 at half the projected annual volume of shipping.

Today the State Thruway Authority runs the canal system as a "recreationway." Since 1995, the state has invested over $100 million in revitalizing the canal system for pleasure boats and hiking, and has set up a Canal Corporation subsidiary to run the show. In 2006, the Canal Corporation's budget was $80 million,[6] while the federal budget for cleaning up all thirty-one Areas of Concern in the eight Great Lakes states was less than half that.

So the Erie Canal is not commercially self-sustaining, and its continued operation is relatively expensive. But it is there. Why not invest in it as a recreationway?

In 1819, construction of the Erie Canal mired to a full stop at Montezuma Swamp, after up to a thousand diggers died there from malaria. Eventually, the state solved this problem by building an aqueduct to carry part of the canal and channeling the Seneca River, cutting the wetlands off from the seasonal overflows that sustained them. The canal, and its successive "improvements," drained the wetlands, imperiling countless native species that coevolved with the natural hydrology of central New York and favoring the spread of nonnative species like the parasitic sea lamprey and the alewife. These invaders now threaten highly valued but struggling populations of prized native fish like lake trout and whitefish throughout the Great Lakes by attaching to and feeding on the adults or eating the fry.

In 1937, the Citizens Conservation Corps began a public works project to restore some of the Montezuma wetlands by building 6.5 miles of dikes to impound water. Restoration continues today through additions of marginal agricultural lands under the North American Waterfowl Management Plan. With minimal management, these restored wetlands support the growing niche in the state's recreation economy for Great Lakes sport fishing and wildlife watching, which brings more people outdoors in New York State than hunting and fishing combined. Nationally, according to a 2006 U.S. Fish and Wildlife Service survey, 31 percent of Americans report wildlife watching as an activity they pursue, spending $45 billion on trips and equipment and supporting over one million jobs.[7]

Thus, before we continue to invest public funds in the Erie Canal at the current rate, we should evaluate the comparative costs of its maintenance, its damages to natural river and wetland functions, its potential as a vector into the upper Great Lakes for nonnative invasive species, and the impact of all this on wildlife and wildlife watching, a significant part of the state's economy.

THE QUEST TO DELIST

IN JULY 2006, the Oswego River became the first U.S. Great Lakes Area of Concern to be officially delisted. Twenty years earlier, the International Joint Commission listed the Oswego on the basis of four known and five more possible "beneficial use impairments." One of these, "restrictions on fish and wildlife consumption" due mainly to PCBs, mirex, and dioxin, affects not only the river but the whole of Lake Ontario, which has one of the most severe health advisories for women of childbearing age and children under fifteen. "Eat *no fish* taken from Lake Ontario and its tributaries to the first impassable barrier." Two other use impairments, "loss of fish and wildlife habitat" and "degradation of fish and wildlife populations," are ascribed to a seasonal half-mile stretch of dry riverbed around the Varick Dam in the city of Oswego.

Beyond restoring these beneficial uses, a federal and state Fisheries Enhancement Plan identified five long-term goals for the river, including restoration of three historic fish species: Lake sturgeon, Atlantic salmon, and American eel.[8] We are far from reaching these long-term goals, nor have we restored at least two of the river's basic beneficial uses—supplying fish that are safe to eat and year-round fish passage at the Varick Dam.

So why was the Oswego River delisted?

Proponents of delisting argued that contaminated fish are a Lake Ontario problem and should be dealt with by a lakewide forum, while the dewatering of the river is a hydrodam problem that should be dealt with through the dam relicensing process. This is a little like the local doctor telling you that because he hasn't the treatments to cure you, you're cured. Then again, in a 2002 report to Congress, the U.S. General Accounting Office faulted the EPA and the Great Lakes states for inaction on their Remedial Action Plans. Something had to be done to show progress.

Ironically, the politics of listing/delisting could wind up a zero sum game for the Oswego, since there are those who want to add Onondaga Lake, one of the river's major source waters and the nation's only Superfund lake, to the list of Great Lakes Areas of Concern.

THE STORY OF ONONDAGA LAKE

CENTURIES BEFORE Jacques Cartier sailed up the St. Lawrence River to Montréal, another stranger, a man of Huron origin, sailed across Lake Ontario in a stone canoe "to spread the New Mind" among the warring nations to the south. The story of the Peacemaker, as told by Paul Wallace in *The White Roots of Peace*, centers on Onondaga Lake.[9]

After converting Jikonsahseh in the west, the Peacemaker (Wallace refers to him as Deganawidah) traveled toward the rising sun and came to the house of the "man who eats humans." He climbed to the roof and waited "until the man came home carrying a human body, which he put in his kettle on the fire. Deganawidah moved closer and looked straight down."

> At that moment the man bent over the kettle. Seeing a face looking up at him, he was amazed. It was Deganawidah's face he saw reflected in the water, but the man thought it was his own. There was in it such wisdom and strength as he had never seen before nor ever dreamed that he possessed. The man moved back into a corner of the house, and sat down and began to think.

So began Hiawatha's transformation to Good Mind. Hiawatha and the Peacemaker eventually persuaded the other nations to stop the blood feuds, all except the Onondaga chief, Atotarho, "for his mind was twisted and his workings were evil and indirect." Atotarho's wizardry caused the death of Hiawatha's wife and three daughters. In his grief, Hiawatha wandered to the Tully Lakes (south of Syracuse) where he picked up mussel shells and began to thread them on rushes while speaking words of condolence to himself. The Peacemaker overheard and used these same words to help clear Hiawatha's mind. With the other chiefs they returned to Onondaga Lake to overcome Atotarho with their message of the New Mind.

> They all put their canoes into the lake and paddled across. As they neared the middle they heard the voice of Atotarho rush out to meet them, crying, "Asonke-ne-e-e-e-eh! It is not yet!" The wind lifted the waves against the canoes, but they put their strength into their paddles and, before the voice had died away, they stood before Atotarho.
>
> "Behold!" said Deganawidah. "Here is Power. These are the Five Nations. Their strength is greater than thy strength. But their voice shall be thy voice when thou speakest in council, and all men shall hear thee. This shall be thy strength in future: the will of a united people."
>
> Then the mind of Atotarho was made straight and Hiawatha combed the snakes out of his hair . . .
>
> Then Deganawidah placed antlers on the heads of the chiefs in sign of their authority, and gave them the Words of the Law. (WRP, 29)

Thus is Onondaga Lake, the place of that first council, sacred to the Haudenosaunee Confederacy.

THE CITY OF SYRACUSE was settled because of Onondaga Lake. The two mainstays of the city's economy in the early 1800s were salt production from brine deposits near the lake and tourism from the lavish resorts for swimming, boating, and fishing all around the lake. Legendary populations of prized Onondaga Lake whitefish and Atlantic salmon inhabited the 4½-mile long, cold water lake.

In the 1880s, production of washing soda (sodium carbonate) began on Onondaga Lake thanks to the local availability of limestone, sodium chloride (salt deposits), and water for processing and disposal. Sodium carbonate is a basic industrial chemical, forming a highly alkaline solution in water that is used in making glass, soaps, wood pulp, and other chemicals. In 1946, sodium chloride became the basis for manufacturing chlorine, another industrial chemical that would have widespread effects in the Great Lakes region.

Allied Chemical and Dye Corporation (now Honeywell International, Inc.) began chlorine production using an electrolysis process requiring mercury cells or batteries to separate the chlorine from the sodium chloride. Between 1946 and 1970, when it closed, the Syracuse chlor-alkili plant dumped an estimated 165,000 pounds of mercury into Onondaga Lake, which became dispersed throughout the lake sediments. In 1995, Onondaga became the first lake to be listed on the National Priorities List as a Superfund site. A dozen subsites around the lake are also listed.

More local chemical manufacturing grew from the chlorine industry, leading to discharges of benzene, toluene, xylene, chlorobenzene, PAHs, PCBs, phenols, cadmium, and other heavy metals to the lake. Twelve hundred acres of wastebeds on the west shore contributed large quantities of chloride, sodium, and calcium to Onondaga Lake, preventing any plant or animal life from taking root. Bristol-Squibb discharged antibiotics, which interfered with sewage bacterial treatment until the company finally built a pretreatment plant. On top of all this, forty combined sewer overflows discharged to the lake; 20 percent of its inflow was said to be treated wastewater.[10]

In 2005, the EPA and the state DEC released a proposed Remedial Action Plan for Onondaga Lake. In response, the Onondaga Nation filed fifty pages of comments, saying the plan was not sufficiently protective of human health and the environment. They noted, for example, that while the plan calls for removing surface contaminants, it leaves behind high concentrations of mercury and other contaninants just below the dredge cut—"a risky strategy that does not appear to be rooted in scientific analysis or good public policy."[11]

Anticipating that these comments would be ignored, they also filed a lawsuit on March 11, 2005, claiming ownership of and responsibility for a swath of land from the shore of eastern Lake Ontario south to the Pennsylvania border (roughly shaded in on the map at the beginning of this chapter). The suit demands a voice in major policy discussions affecting that land, especially Onondaga Lake. The opening statement of this lawsuit reaches back to the Peacemaker and forward to the next generations:

> The Nation and its people have a unique relationship with the
> land, which is embodied in *Gayanashagowa,* the Great Law of

Peace. This relationship goes far beyond federal and state legal concepts of ownership, possession, or other legal rights. The people are one with the land and consider themselves stewards of it. It is the duty of the Nation's leaders to work for a healing of this land, to protect it, and to pass it on to future generations.

In the fall of 2005, I joined a bus tour around Onondaga Lake led by Ed Michalenko, of the Onondaga Lake Improvement Corporation, and by members of the Haudenosaunee Environmental Task Force who were hosting their tenth annual Indian Nation Leaders conference in Syracuse to make their concerns known to federal and state government representatives. I had been on many tours of toxic hotspots around the Great Lakes—the Detroit River, Love Canal, the Fox River at Green Bay—but this was, at least visually, the grimmest. A crusty, barren, lunar landscape of salty wastebeds stretching, in places, as far as the eye could see dominated the west side of the lake, where the industries concentrated. Earthmovers were everywhere, scraping here, building barriers and berms there, in an attempt to control the flow of contaminants. It was raining hard, making the whole effort look even more futile.

I asked the Onondaga woman who was sitting in front of me on the bus what she thought. "Even with a better plan, do you really think restoring this lake is possible?"

She smiled and said, "Of course. We wouldn't be here if it wasn't."

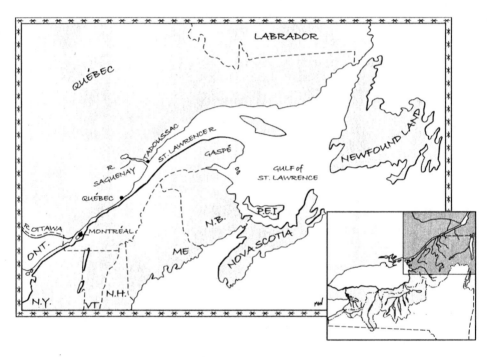

9.1 Le Fleuve

NINE

LE FLEUVE

And now through the present expedition undertaken at
your royal command for the discovery of lands in the west
formerly unknown to you and to us, lying in the same cli-
mates and parallels as your territories and kingdom, you will
learn and hear of their fertility and richness, of the immense
number of peoples living there, of their kindness and peace-
fulness, and likewise of the richness of the great river, which
flows through and waters the midst of these lands of yours,
which is without comparison the largest river that is known
to have ever been seen.

—Jacques Cartier, *Dedication to King Francis I*

As the right of each sentient species to live in accordance
with its normal cultural evolution is considered sacred, no
Star Trek personnel may interfere with the healthy development of alien life and culture . . . even to save their lives
and/or their ships.

—*Star Trek*, "The Prime Directive"

QUÉBEQUOIS ARE NOT HAPPY CAMPERS in the Great Lakes environmental movement. "No pollution without representation!," they shout
at International Joint Commission (IJC) public meetings, pointing out
that Québec should be party to the Great Lakes Water Quality Agreement—like the province of Ontario, the eight bordering Great Lakes
states, and the two countries—especially since the St. Lawrence River is
at the receiving end of so many Great Lakes water quality problems.[1]

But the agreement adheres to a definition of the Great Lakes ecosystem that includes only a small part of the river, the 100 miles or so that serve as an international border. And the IJC, who oversees the agreement, was set up by the Boundary Waters Treaty of 1909 specifically to monitor only those waters shared by the United States and Canada.

So maps of the Great Lakes ecosystem tend to be cropped on the right at Cornwall/Massena, while the St. Lawrence River runs on for another 650 francophone miles to the sea. Who knew there was so much more river there? Who knows how much more we have to learn from our bristly neighbors to the Northeast, all of whom, as their license plates so provocatively say, *remember.*

Je me souviens.

Remember what? Ah, but now they have you. While I believe it means that every *habitant,* or at least every one with a licensed vehicle, remembers back to before 1763 when the Treaty of Paris gave Canada to Great Britain, to when all of Canada and major parts of America were French, it suggests so much more. It suggests that Québec is holding on to things that everyone else has forgotten, including one of the principal rivers of North America.

About the St. Lawrence, the raison d'être of French Canada, the first thing to remember is this: ce n'est pas *une riviére,* c'est *un fleuve*—a *big river,* by far the largest in the Great Lakes system. Ninety miles wide at its mouth, the river in its last several hundred miles is really an inland arm of the sea, an estuary up to the Saguenay River, its first major tributary. Upstream from the estuary, the St. Lawrence remains tidal as far as Québec City, and predominantly salt water all the way in to Trois-Rivières. Above Trois Rivières, a step or two rise from sea level, the Great Lakes prevail with their legacy of glacial meltwater and their distilling rains helping to keep the sweet water sweet.

Thus, for much of its length, the St. Lawrence River is a graduated mixing zone providing a set of unique ecological niches between fresh and saltwater. Parts of it have evolved their own endemic subspecies, including the signature species of the estuary, the St. Lawrence beluga whale, a distinct population of an estimated 1,200 animals that live here and nowhere else in the world. Atlantic salmon, American eel, and other fish also depend on the river as a link between the sweet and seawater habitats they need to complete their life cycles.

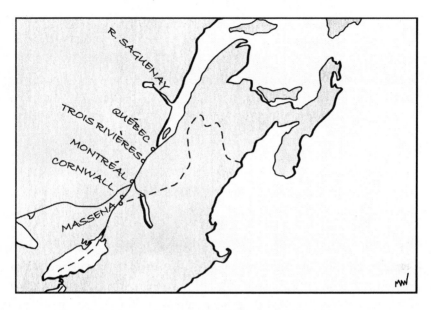

9.2. ST. LAWRENCE RIVER MIXING ZONE

As a navigation channel—Amerindians called it "the road that walks"—le Fleuve Saint-Laurent was Europe's major entryway into North America, and continues to be a major conduit for nonnative species. In 1535, Jacques Cartier sailed and then longboated up the St. Lawrence as far as present-day Montréal. From there, "the most violent rapid it is possible to see" (later named the Lachine or "China" Rapids humoring France's single-minded quest for Asia) blocked his advance further upstream. With its completion in 1959, the St. Lawrence Seaway bypassed the Lachine Rapids along with other impediments to seagoing vessels, and Asia itself came to the Great Lakes in the form of trans-oceanic ships containing microaquatic species in their ballast waters.

Many nonnative species have established themselves in Great Lakes waters in this way, including the pistachio-sized zebra mussel, first found in Lake St. Clair in 1988, and the related quagga mussel that showed up about a decade later, both thought to have hitchhiked in from the Caspian Sea. Beyond costing some $5 billion in efforts to control their damages to utility pipes and pumps, these mussels have pushed many species of native mussels to the brink of extinction. They are also suspect in two scourges on Lake Erie: the central basin "dead zone" and an avian botulism epidemic that has killed thousands of loons and other fish-eating birds in the eastern basin since 1999. Both events have been linked to nutrient loading and contaminant mobilization related to the explosive population dynamics of these mollusks in an extremely out-of-balance aquatic ecosystem. By U.S. Geological Survey calculations, a new exotic species enters the Great Lakes via ballast water from foreign ships on average once every eight months.[2]

Le Fleuve, in short, walks two ways, which is all the more reason why Québec, geographically stationed at the eastern door, should be party to any international arrangements attempting to protect the Great Lakes ecosystem.

IN THE SUMMER OF 2005, my Toronto friend Maureen and I set out to explore the St. Lawrence, following the river downstream from our homes and stomping grounds in the lower Great Lakes, while reading Cartier's accounts of sailing upstream almost half a millenium earlier.[3] From first hail to final expulsion, Cartier's *Voyages* reads like the case study that might have led to *Star Trek*'s Prime Directive, an intergalactic ethic conceived, if not practiced, in the wake of cultural collisions such as that between sixteenth-century France and *Haudenausenega*. On our car-camping voyage we too are immersed in another culture, though it occupies a river much changed from the one Cartier "discovered." The one constant we share is the river road itself, which continues to walk between alien worlds.

THE SEAWAY

OUR GOAL IS THE Saguenay River, with the possibility of going all the way out to the ChicChoc Mountains, the northern end of the Appalachian Range on the Gaspé Peninsula, if we can explore that far and back in ten days. We've met Québec climbers in the Adirondacks who have "done the ChicChocs" and said they are *magnifique* and *incroyable*. (Learn to pronounce these two superlatives just so and you can go far in Québec on your high school French.) The Gaspé Penin-sula forms the lower lip of the river's mouth on the Gulf of St.

Lawrence, which extends the sweet-saltwater interface another 250 miles further east to Newfoundland, North America's final Atlantic frontier at this parallel.

From Whiteface Mountain in the Adirondacks, it's about a two-hour drive north to Montréal, second-largest francophone city in the world, and the major port of call on the St. Lawrence Seaway.

The seaway dominates the first 150 miles of river between Lake Ontario and Montréal, where the natural river, including the Thousand Islands, was once too narrow, too shallow, and too steep to be navigated. In a joint construction project (1954–1959), Canada and the United States created a uniform 27-foot-deep shipping channel along this stretch by blasting and dredging out two million tons of rocks and earth, and building seven locks, numerous canals, and the international Moses-Saunders Dam that controls water levels not only in the St. Lawrence River, but across Lake Ontario.

The proposed seaway never underwent an environmental impact assessment. It was justified by expectations that it would benefit regional and national economies by opening inland Great Lakes ports to international trade and facilitating cost-effective internal transport of bulk goods like grain, iron ore, and coal.

These expectations never fully materialized. International traffic accounts for less than 7 percent of seaway trade, and domestic shipping has declined steadily over the past two decades.[4] The entire operation was and is heavily subsidized by both governments. The codevelopment of hydropower at the Moses-Saunders Dam brought industries attracted by cheap electricity and waste disposal options, just as it did on the Niagara Frontier, including aluminum smelters, foundries, chemical manufacturers, and pulp and paper mills, along with their various associated dumps. In the words of Akwesasne writer Bruce Johansen, it transformed "a natural paradise to an environmental hell."[5]

In the last decade, the need to relicense the Moses-Saunders power dam for another fifty years, along with an Army Corps of Engineers' proposal to significantly enlarge the navigation channel in the river, initiated a reevaluation of the seaway's relative costs and benefits. The Corps released its *Great Lakes Navigation System Review* in 2003, suggesting that with 35 feet of draft throughout the navigation system and with larger locks, the seaway could realize significant new container ship cargo. Critics replied that any improvements to the seaway should focus on domestic and Canada/U.S. trade, which accounts for 93 percent of its use. A regional focus would eliminate this vector for new introductions of aquatic invasive species, would better fit the natural capacity of Great Lakes navigation channels, and would cost the environment and the taxpayers much less.

The Mohawk communities of Akwesasne/St. Regis (immediately downstream from the power dam) and Kahnawaké (closer to Montréal), provided lengthy testimony on the impacts of the project to the river and to their way of life, such as these words from Haundenosaunee Environmental Task Force member James Ransom:

> Before the Project, the elders tell us you could see twenty to thirty feet into the waters. Today the waters are muddied and visibility is cloudy. Access to many of our islands, such as Yellow Island and St. Regis Island could be achieved in the summer time by walking through the shallow waters of the river. Now the river is too deep and the current is too fast. Our people took their drinking water directly from the river. Instead we have to rely on drilled wells, many of them containing high sulfur and iron that renders them unfit for drinking.
>
> Mohawk lands located west of the dam were taken from our people and flooded. We know that fishing holes in the St. Lawrence River within our territories were filled in with dredged materials . . . We know that the physical structures of the Project prevent the movement of fish up and down the river.
>
> We have seen many species of fish, once abundant in the river, virtually disappear. The remaining species east of the Project have become contaminated with PCBs, mercury and heavy metals. The Project's three local power users, and the greatest beneficiaries of the Project, are the sources of this contamination . . . Today, fishing advisories tell our women of child-bearing age, infants, and children under the age of sixteen to eat no fish at all from the St. Lawrence River.
>
> The health of our community, like the health of the river, has deteriorated greatly.[6]

9.3. ST. LAWRENCE SEAWAY REGION

Before crossing the bridge to Montréal, Maureen and I detour a
mile or two west to view the seaway at Kahnawaké, whose population—7,087 individuals in 2005, according to the *Québec Aboriginal
Tourist Guide*—"has been located near the Lachine rapids on the south
shore of the St. Lawrence since the 18th century [and] has been forced
to adapt to the constant development of the surrounding cities."

That is an understatement. Approaching Kahnawaké by land
requires running the gauntlet of a commercial strip so out-of-control it
seems punitive. We find ourselves in bumper-to-bumper traffic speeding
through a curbless, laneless jungle of signs held up on sticks: Discount
liquor? Fried chicken? Auto parts? It's hard to say. We cannot see the

trees for the forest. Eventually, and only because we are really looking for it, we see a little board bearing the word, "Kahnawaké" and pointing diagonally right. We veer off and pass through a small culvert under the bridge to Montréal, which immediately slows us down to the limit on Main Street, 15 miles per hour, enforced by a stop sign on every corner.

Suddenly, we are in another world.

Kahnawaké is 60 miles downstream from the Moses-Saunders power dam and its surrounding industries. At first we don't even see the seaway. We wend our way slowly through quiet streets toward the river, here a low and narrow canal running behind "downtown," behind an old and worn residential neighborhood, behind a shrine enclosing the bones of Kateri Tekakwitha (1656–1680), Kahnawaké's most famous resident, beatified in 1980 but still awaiting sainthood. Then, miraculously, from the shadow of the senior citizen center and towering over it, the *Ziema* appears, hailing from Monrovia. She glides silently and quickly through the backyards, heading out to the Atlantic. No one but us is out in Kahnawaké to hail it. We wave, but see no one on board to wave back.

We turn back to the traffic jam leading to the bridge to the city once known to the Haudenosaunee as Hochelega, renamed *Mount Royal* by Cartier in 1535. A mountain island city in the midst of the St. Lawrence, already at the latitude of northern Wisconsin (though the river itself has so much farther north to go), Montréal in winter recalls how glaciers begin, how Cartier's ships froze, how his men died of scurvy, how tough life is.

But in July Montréal is an outdoor theater, a continuous performance art of, by, and for the people. We easily could scrap our plans and spend our ten days on Rue Saint-Denis. Here we discover a native food, *poutine*, a heady mix of French fries, melted cheese curds, gravy, and ketchup, and a festival, *Juste pour Rire* (Just for Laughs), in full swing. Acrobats and bawdy operettas, puppets two-stories high, and women on stilts in full Louis Quatorze drag have taken over the streets. The festival will go on for a week, to be followed by another, the Festival of Twins, well worth waiting for, or so everyone says, but no, we stick to the plan and head east out of town, hoping to find a place to camp near the river by nightfall.

CARTIER'S FIRST VOYAGE

JACQUES CARTIER sailed into the Gulf of St. Lawrence in 1534 with two ships, sixty sailors, and a mandate from King Francis I to (a) find a route to Cathay and (b) take whatever gold and treasure lay along the way, such as Cortez had "found" for Spain. It took him just twenty days to cross the Atlantic from the coast of Brittany, following a route already well known to French and Scandinavian fishermen. He traveled through the strait separating Newfoundland from Labrador, ranged southwest across the Gulf to Prince Edward Island, then nosed his way north along the east coast, looking for a way to penetrate the continent. He did not discover the St. Lawrence River on this, the first of his three voyages, and he found no wealth, but he did not return empty-handed either.

In mid-July, bad weather forced Cartier's two ships to harbor in the bay south of the Gaspé peninsula for eleven days. They already had encountered two groups of native people who had hailed them from shore—the first, "holding up to us some skins on sticks," advertising their desire to trade. Now, while Cartier waited out the fog and wind in Gaspé Bay, "there arrived a large number of savages . . . not at all of the same race or language of the first we met," who had come to fish for mackerel. These turned out to be St. Lawrence Iroquois, whose principal village, Stadacona (near present-day Québec City), lay about 500 miles upstream. "When they had mixed with us a little on shore, they came freely in their canoes to the sides of our vessels" and traded for knives, glass beads, and trinkets. Always the sharp trader, Cartier observed "the whole lot of them had not anything above the value of five sous, their canoes and fishing nets excepted" (C24).

On July 24, the day before they would depart, the French erected a 30-foot cross at the entrance to Gaspé Harbor, which provoked the Iroquois chief, Donnacona, along with three sons and a brother, to approach the ships in his canoe. "[P]ointing to the cross he made us a long harangue, making the sign of the cross with two of his fingers, and then he pointed to the land all around about, as if he wished to say that all this region belonged to him, and that we ought not to have set up this cross without his permission."

Cartier's men held up an ax, "pretending we would barter it for his skin." When Donnacona's canoe came close enough, they seized it and two of his sons.

> [We] made them come on board our vessel at which they were greatly astonished . . . And then we explained to them by signs that the cross had been set up to serve as a landmark and guidepost on coming into the harbour, and that we would soon come back and would bring them iron wares and other goods; and that we wished to take two of his sons away with us and afterwards would bring them back again to that harbour. (C26–27)

And so Cartier did not return to France empty-handed, but with two captive Iroquois, thereby setting a course that would contribute to the failure of his next two expeditions and possibly to the disappearance of the Stadaconan Iroquois from the river.

QUÉBEC AND THE PRIME DIRECTIVE

WE FOLLOW ROUTE 138 along the north shore of the St. Lawrence River, stop briefly for maps at Trois Rivières and navigate through rush hour traffic around Québec City, whose natural advantages as a fortress are obvious even from the road. The city occupies high ground overlooking the river where it narrows to less than a mile wide. "Kebec" says the *Aboriginal Guide*, means "where the stream is obstructed." The battle for the St. Lawrence River, the climactic battle of the French and Indian Wars, was fought here in 1759. General Montcalm and General Wolfe both died on Québec's Plains of Abraham, and Canada fell to the British.

Je me souviens.

We can find no place to camp by the river, but day is ending, so, just beyond Baie St. Paul, we turn north on Route 381 and head for a national park in the Charlevoix Mountains. As the road climbs, the mountains become more desolate—bare rock, thin soils, scorched skeletons of trees. We learn from a SEPAQ (Société des établissements de plein air du Québec) brochure that there has been a succession of fires, the most recent in 1999. But the "devastation" we see is also due to the fact that the forest here is taiga, which, by definition, means bare rock, thin soils, sparse trees. The campsites are austere: little squares of gravel to pitch your tent on, no soft earth, no pine needles, and absolutely no fires allowed.

Next morning we climb a steep path through black spruce trees bearded with long white lichen to the top of Mont du Lac des Cygnes from where we can see the St. Lawrence River 25 miles to the south. Northern Maine is just another 40 miles or so beyond the river's southern shore. In the Adirondacks we often have mountain summits to ourselves. But, up here, there must be at least fifty people, and a gorgeous Amazonian summit warden with long brown braids instructing them not to step on the fragile Arctic plants. She explains to us with a set of pictures that the valley below is a giant meteor crater, one of the ten largest in the world.

Incroyable, we say.

On the way down we meet two women climbing up.

The one in front is smiling excitedly. She puts up her finger: "Ssssh!"

We stop. Between us a large black chicken–like bird steps on to the trail and slowly begins to inflate. Its color changes to speckled white as its underpinnings ruff up. Its tail fans like a peacock's, showing a soft brown edge and large white spots. For several minutes it turns slowly like a *tai chi* master, occasionally snapping its fan to keep us focused. We take pictures.

Then it disappears into the brush on the other side of the trial.

"Tetra," declares the woman in front, heading past us.

"Huh?," we say.

"Tetra! TETRA!," she says louder to our blankness, the magic of our little interspecies moment broken by this failure to understand one of our own.

Back at the campsite, we consult my Audubon field guide, which says it is a spruce grouse, genus *tetraonidae*; it adds, by way of a personal note: "This northern grouse is extraordinarily tame and can occasionally be approached and killed with a stick."

Later, camping at *Le Bic*, another national park on the south shore of the St. Lawrence, we learn more about Québec's version of the

Prime Directive. Entering *Le Bic* is like coming into a high-end refugee camp. Cars, tents, and extended families with babies and old folks sprawl across a grassy parking lot next to the highway. And again, unlike the Adirondacks where we are sometimes the sole occupants of state parks, this field is crowded. SEPAQ has reserved the good spots—the forested hills, the flowered meadows, the pretty bays along the river—for resident wildlife. We hike to the river at dawn to breakfast alone with harbor seals and are grateful that the small city of people just now waking up and happily heading for their 30-second, two-loony showers is miles back at the highway.

CARTIER' SECOND VOYAGE

ON MAY 19, 1535, Cartier left his homeport of St. Malo with three vessels, one hundred and ten Frenchmen, and Donnacona's two sons, Dom Agaya and Taignoagny. On August 10, they arrived at a bay on the north shore of the Gulf of St. Lawrence.

> The two savages assured us that this was the way to the mouth of the great river of Hochelega and the route towards Canada, and that the river grew narrower as one approached Canada; and also that farther up, the water became fresh, and that one could make one's way so far up the river that they had never heard of anyone reaching the head of it. (C45)

It was the feast day of St. Lawrence and so they named the river. Finding Hochelega had become the purpose of this second voyage, just as finding the "Kingdom of Saguenay" would be the mission of the third. Both were destinations on an imaginery map shaped by France's desire for Asia as detailed by Cartier's limited understanding of his native guides and their limited understanding of him.

When they reached Stadecona (Québec City) and were rejoined with their people, Cartier's "two savages" began behaving, he thought, strangely. They were "altogether changed in their attitude and goodwill, and refused to come on board our ships, although many times begged to do so. At this we began somewhat to distrust them"(C52). They reneged on their promise to guide him upstream to Hochelega, and their father,

Donnacona, not only refused but tried everything in his means to prevent it. First he said they would not guide him any further as the river was not worth exploring. Cartier said he would go on without them. Then the Iroquois leader sent the French captain three children—a ten-year-old girl and two younger boys—as a gift "with the intent he should not go to Hochelega." Cartier put the children on board his ship, but said, nevertheless, that he must go. Finally, after the French gave a demonstration of their firepower by ordering "a dozen cannon to be fired with their bullets into the wood that stood opposite to the ships and the people," Donnacona invoked his own higher power.

As Cartier describes it, "Donnacona, Taignoagny and the others devised a ruse, and dressed up three men as devils, who pretended to be sent from their god Cudouagny, to prevent us from going to Hochelega" (C55). They said these men brought tidings from Hochelega "that there would be so much ice and snow that all would perish." At this the Frenchmen laughed, saying, "Jesus would keep them safe from the cold if they would trust him," and the next day they set sail up the river. This was September 19, 1535.

For the next two weeks, they navigated first by ship, then by longboat, through Lake St. Pierre and past many villages. Cartier catalogued the plants and animals he recognized, including the fish of the river.

> Moreover, you will find in this river in June, July and August great numbers of mackerel, mullets, maigres, tunnies, large-sized eels, and other fish, When their [spawning] season is over you will find as good smelts as in the river Seine. In spring again there are quantities of lampreys and salmons. Up above Canada are many pike, trout, carp, breams, and other fresh-water fish. All these varieties are caught, each in its season, in considerable quantities by these people for their food and sustenance. (C 74–75)

Note that this first reference to "Canada" was based on another misunderstanding. "As the Frenchmen inquired the names of the villages along the banks, a reply which they commonly received from their two Indian guides was the word *Canada*, which is simply the Mohawk word for 'village.' Hence Cartier naturally got the impression that Canada was the name of the river or country through which it flowed."[7]

On October 2, they arrived at Hochelega where "came to meet us more than a thousand persons, men, women and children, who . . . brought us great quantities of fish, and of their bread which is made of corn, throwing so much of it into our longboats that it seemed to rain bread"(C59). Historians read this magnanimous reception as signifying that it was the Hochelegans' first contact with Europeans.

Here the land was cultivated "with large fields covered with the corn of the country" and, in the midst of these fields, there was a village of fifty longhouses encircled by three tiers of wooden walls. The people carried out their paralyzed chief and others who were sick or injured or "so extremely old that their eyelids hung down to their cheeks" in order that Cartier "might lay his hands upon them, so that one would have thought Christ had come down on earth to heal them"(C64). The captain set about rubbing the chief's arms and legs, read aloud from a prayer book, distributed the usual hatchets, knives, beads, and other small trinkets, and then went on to climb the mountain he had already named "Mount Royal."

From the summit of Mount Royal, Cartier first saw the Lachine Rapids, most definitively blocking this way to China. Not one to be deterred, he turned to the guides with his question—Which way then?—and their quick and canny response allowed him to replace the dream of Hochelega with the dream of Saguenay.

> [They] showed us furthermore that along the mountains to the north there is a large river, which comes from the west . . . We thought this river [Ottawa] must be the one that flows through the kingdom and province of Saguenay, and without our asking any questions or making any sign, they seized the chain of the Captain's whistle, which was made of silver, and a dagger-handle of yellow copper-gilt like gold . . . and gave us to understand that these came from up that river. (C65)

Donnacona and his sons would add fuel to this fire, placing on Cartier's mental map of the fabulous Kingdom of Saguenay the details they must have thought he most required to hear: details that might finally rid them of him; details that Cartier determined the King of France should hear from their own authentic lips.

And they gave us to understand that in that country the people go clothed and dressed in woollens like ourselves; that there are many towns and peoples composed of honest folk who possess great store of gold and copper. Furthermore . . . that beyond the [kingdom of the] Saguenay, this tributary flows through two or three large, very broad lakes, until one reaches a fresh-water sea, of which there is no mention of anyone having seen the bounds, as the people of Saguenay had informed them; for they themselves, they told us, had never been there. (C75–76)

After Hochelega, Cartier sailed back downstream to his base camp on the St. Charles River in the region of Stadecona to find that, so badly had relations with Donnacona's people degenerated, his men had built a fort in front of the ships "with artillery pointing every way." He blamed "the two rogues," Taignoagny and Dom Agaya, for the "certain coldness between us." Thus began the famous winter of 1535 and 1536, during which, it might be said, Cudouagny's prophecy was realized.

From the middle of November until the fifteenth of April, we lay frozen up in ice, which was more than two fathoms thick, while on shore were more than four feet of snow . . . with the result that all our beverages froze in their casks. And all about the decks of the ships, below hatches and above, there was ice to the depth of four finger breaths. And the whole river was frozen where the water was fresh up to Hochelega. (C79)

Twenty-five seamen died of scurvy before they learned the cure of boiled white cedar leaves and bark from Dom Agaya. This was so effective that the surviving sailors not only immediately felt better and began to recover strength, but also "were cured of all the diseases they had ever had," including the French pox.

When this became known, there was such a press for the medicine that they almost killed each other to have it first; so that in less than eight days a whole tree as large and as tall as any I ever saw was used up . . . and produced such a result that . . . all the drugs of Alexandria could not have done so much in a year as did this tree in eight days. (C80)

Meanwhile another "pestilence"—presumably not scurvy as they already knew the cure—killed more than fifty people at Stadecona.

The next few pages of the *Voyages* tell a story of mounting intrigue and fear of attack on both sides. Cartier was determined to kidnap Donnacona "that he might relate and tell to the king all he had seen in the west of the wonders of the world" (C82). Taignoagny informed Cartier's spies "that if the Captain would do him a good turn and would seize a leader of that region named Agona, who had slighted him and would carry him off to France, that he (Taignoagny) would be in Cartier's debt and would do anything he asked" (C82). Cartier refused. He would take no adults, only children. "The Captain spoke thus in order to calm their fears and to induce Donnacona, who still kept on the other side of the river, to cross over. Taignoagny was much pleased at these words, which made him hope he should never go back to France" (C83). He returned the next day with his father, his brother, and two other headmen, all of whom were promptly seized by Cartier's men.

And so Cartier returned to France, in May 1536, with ten native people, including the five kidnapped men and five "gift" children, all of whom would die over the next four years in France, except for one little girl who lived on, though she never returned to North America.

She could narrate the film that has yet to be made. *Je me souviens.*

THE SAGUENAY

The next morning, we made sail and got under way in order to push forward, and discovered a species of fish, which none of us had ever seen or heard of. This fish is large as a porpoise but has no fin. It is very similar to a greyhound about the body and head and is as white as snow, without a spot upon it. Of these there are a very large number in this river, living between the salt and fresh water. The people of this country call them *Adhothuys* and told us they are very good to eat. They also informed us that these fish are found nowhere else in all this river and country except at this spot. (C48)

CARTIER'S "FISH" is none other than the St. Lawrence beluga whale, the object of this leg of our journey. We are approaching the estuary and the Saguenay River, one of the best places in the world to see whales. Twelve cetacean species, including the blue whale, the largest mammal on earth, visit the St. Lawrence estuary seasonally. One species, the beluga, lives there year-round, and in July can be found in large numbers, no one knows quite why, in the Saguenay River. The Saguenay also has its own distinct populations of at least seventeen other arctic species, dating back to when the last glacier melted, and the St. Lawrence Valley, still depressed from its weight, was invaded by the sea and its creatures all the way in to Lake Ontario.

A torrential rainfall forces us off the road for awhile, but now the sky is lifting and we are following Route 138 down a hill into the village of St. Siméon.

"Bienvenue a St. Siméon, whale capital of the world," says Maureen, reading a billboard, while I scan the sweep of river, spread below and to the right of us.

Sure enough, a long black back surfaces in the smooth water a half-mile out from shore. We join a few others at the bottom of the hill who are picnicking and watching two feeding humpback whales. We will learn later that four cetacean species have been spotted this July in the estuary, including humpbacks, blue whales, five sperm whales (the same species as Moby Dick), and, of course, belugas.

At the mouth of the Saguenay River, between the villages of Baie St. Catherine and Tadoussac, Route 138 simply continues for about 15 minutes as a free ferry ride. This ferry shunts back and forth all day, the only link for 70 miles between the parts of Québec on either side of the Saguenay. *Why not a bridge?* Now we begin to learn what makes this tributary so unique. Technically, it is a *fjord*, a drowned river valley surrounded by mountains whose steep-walled sides dive 400 feet below the waterline at the mouth. From a whale's perspective, the inflowing ocean hits a wall at Tadoussac, sending it up the Saguenay River almost all the way to the northern city of Chicoutimi. Salt and freshwater stack up in the estuary and in the fjord almost to the source of the Saguenay. My Chicoutimi friend, Marc Hudon, describes it thus:

Regarding the salt and freshwater mixture of the Saguenay River . . . the top surface is freshwater and one to ten feet below is the denser saltwater part. It is layered lake that all the way up the river to La Baie and the Chicoutimi where it is only fresh water. Saltwater ends at St. Fulgence.

St. Fulgence is 60 miles upstream from the St. Lawrence River, making the Saguenay one of the longest fjords in the world.

Even if a bridge over the Saguenay was a feasible engineering project, it could prove devastating to the local economy, which depends on tourism, particularly whale-watching. At a whale museum in Tadoussac, we listen through a headset connected to an underwater microphone to hear what the whales are hearing. Between the inflatable Zodiacs carrying half a dozen binoculared passengers and the larger triple-deck cruise boats, the arc of sound ranges from annoying to deafening.[8] The museum encourages whale-watching from shore.

The St. Lawrence belugas, numbering somewhere between 1,000 and 1,400 individuals, are a threatened population, though their numbers have more than doubled since the years when they were pursued and destroyed, not as a food source, but as unwanted competitors for a declining commercial fishery. In those years, they were considered a "nuisance specie" and even bombed from the air. In 1955, hunting belugas became illegal, and the population rallied.

Currently, the population is threatened by high rates of cancer and other diseases caused by contaminants in the fish they consume. Unlike the filter-feeding baleens, belugas are toothed, fish-eating whales—top predators in the St. Lawrence River food chain. A team of wildlife biologists, including former IJC commissioner Pierre Béland, has been researching St. Lawrence belugas since the mid-1980s, largely through autopsies performed on washed-up whales. They have compiled an astonishing list of afflictions—from malignant tumors to organ deformities to widespread bacterial or viral infections—whose common thread appears to be high levels of carcinogenic and hormone-disrupting chemicals found in their fat. Some of the most contaminated individuals are under two years old. Although belugas can live up to forty years, gestation takes twelve to fifteen months, and calves are especially at risk because of the concentrated loads of toxins they receive in the womb and then ingest with mothers' milk.

"By the time a baby beluga stops nursing at two years of age, it will have acquired a toxic load that, relative to its size, far exceeds that of its mother," comments Theo Colborn on these findings. "Béland and his associates found one young whale that had over five hundred parts per million of PCBs in its body—ten times more than the level to qualify as hazardous waste under Canadian law."[9] The research has also linked mirex in the fat of migrating eels to die-offs of St. Lawrence belugas who consume eels in large quantities and whose body burdens of mirex were found to be one hundred times higher than in Arctic populations.[10]

FROM OUR CAMPSITE at Parc National du Saguenay, on the east side of the river just north of Tadoussac, Maureen and I walk 2 miles to a height of land below which belugas are often seen. It's about 7:30 in the morning, foggy and quiet. Before we reach the point, we hear them.

Ooueee?

Hoooh!

Eyi eyi eyi . . .

Their language consists of whistles, clicks, raucous squeals, bell tones, and echolocution or sonar. Humans have not broken the code, though I'm quite sure we are hearing contact calls and warning growls, possibly triggered by our approach. We see two groups feeding and lolling around, mostly all-white adults with a few gray juveniles and at least one small calf, about fifteen in all. A father and his two little boys tiptoe respectfully out to the overlook. The man gives us a long harangue in whispered French. We reply accordingly:

"Magnifique!"

"Incroyable!"

Later, as the fog disperses, freighters start coming down from the industrial port of Baie near Chicoutimi—first the *SPICA*, then the *Federal Venture*—leaving a wake of 2-foot waves bouncing off both sides of the fjord. The whales disappear.

CARTIER'S THIRD VOYAGE

ON MAY 23, 1541, Cartier made his third and last voyage to Terra Nova. This time the captain served under the Lord of Roberval, whom King

Francis had appointed "Lieutenant and Governour of the Countreys of Canada and Hochelega." The purpose of this voyage, besides finding the treasures of Saguenay, was to establish a permanent colony. To that end, they had between them eight ships and a small village of several hundred people, including wives, children, blacksmiths, farmers, vintners, barbers, and some fifty others "recruited" from French prisons, plus a cargo of cattle, goats, hogs, and other animals to breed in the country. For unknown reasons, but presumably because all these arrangements were so complicated, Cartier departed France a year before Roberval.

On August 23, Cartier approached the settlements near Stadecona and was greeted by the people there, including Agona, the apparent leader in Donnacona's absence.

> And after the sayd Agona had inquired of the Captaine where Donnacona and the rest were, the Captaine answered him, That Donnacona was dead in France, and that his body rested in the earth, and that the rest stayed there as great Lords, and were maried, and would not returne back into their Countrey: the said Agona made no shewe of anger at all these speeches: And I think he tooke it so well because he remained Lord and Governour of the country by the death of said Donnacona. (C98)

The text suggests that Cartier lied and Agona's self-interest caused him to pretend to believe. Cartier further omits mention of the fact that Agona's replacement, the French "Lord and Governour of the countrey," would soon arrive.

Cartier set a crew to work building a fort at Cape Rouge, just upstream from Stadacona, and departed with another for Hochelega "of purpose to view and understand the fashion of the *Saults* of water, which are to be passed to goe to Saguenay" (C102). The Lachine Rapids, he found on this second look, were indeed impassble. One can well imagine Cartier's disappointment as William Vollman, in his fictional chronicle, *Fathers and Crows*, imagines Samuel de Champlain's at these same rapids sixty-three years later:

> *This* was no ship-way to China, (And the Golden Kingdom of the Saguenay—what if that too were one of their fairytales?) . . . The Montagnais who had brought him to the rapids

watched his face; they were sorry for him because he was dis-
appointed. To please him, they had agreed with him when he
expressed, disguised as a strictly neutral and hypothetical question, his desperate wish that the Fleuve Saint-Laurent would
take him to the Chinese Sea; after all, he must be a powerful
dreamer to have come across the Great Waters to them. Perhaps
his dreams could make it so for him. And there were many seas
of sweet water in the interior, that they knew.

You have lied to me, said Champlain at last, very coldly . . .
This time tell me the truth, he said. Above these rapids, how
many more?

Twenty more, a Savage said.

And then China?

You will surely find it if you seek it.[11]

Again native people greeted Cartier's boats and guided them along
the way, though now Cartier regarded everything they did with suspi-
cion "for if they thought they had bene too strong for us, then would
they have done their best to have killed us." The fears were mutual:
"And when we were arrived at our Fort, wee understoode by our
people that the Savages of the Country came not any more about our
Fort as they were accustomed, to bring us fish, and that they were in
wonderful doubt and feare of us" (C105).

Cartier's fleet wintered over at Cape Rouge, but started for France
as soon as the ice broke up in spring of 1542. They met Roberval's vessels, just arriving on the coast of Newfoundland, and were ordered by
the latter to return to the fort on the river. But the captain had no
intention of returning and "stole privily away the next night" (C109).
Roberval lost fifty people to disease and another eight to drowning that
winter, and returned to France in spring of 1543. No colonies were
established, and the "Diamants," "leaves of fine gold as thick as a man's
nayle," and quantities of "the best yron in the world" Cartier brought
back to France proved to be worthless.

It was left to Champlain to establish a French colony on the St.
Lawrence River and to navigate up the Ottawa River to Lake Huron,
the main route into the Great Lakes for the next two centuries. When
he arrived in 1603, he confronted many of the same obstacles as

Cartier, particularly the Lachine Rapids. And yet, already, it was a very different river.

> As they approached the Saint Charles they saw no traces of the Iroquoian town of Stadecona. On they went, as far as Hochelega, where Cartier had been entertained sixty-eight years before but not one of its long bark cabins was left, nor a vestige of its stout triple palisade, nor a living soul to tell the story of the dire catastrophe. No Iroquois were now to be met on the St. Lawrence except as invaders.[12]

RUN OF THE RIVER

WE SAVOR THE WHALES in and around the Saguenay for four days, then cross the river—the 35-mile-distance takes 55 minutes on a high-speed car ferry—from Forestville to Ramouski. Seaway investment in Montréal's harbor displaced Ramouski as an inland port, but the city seems to have reinvented itself as Québec's vacationland—gateway to the mountains, the scenic coastline, the art colonies, and the seafood of the Gaspésie.

However, time is up, we have a mission to complete, and the Gaspésie will have to wait. We turn west, back to the engineered upper river to study the impacts of the seaway's power dams.

The first of these, heading upstream, is HydroQuébec's Beauharnois run-of-the-river power plant. Taking advantage of the fall of water at Lachine Rapids, it is the largest electricity-generating station on the St. Lawrence River with an installed capacity of 1,637 megawatts. It is "run-of-the river" because it has no reservoir; the river runs right through it.

Maybe it is because Route 138 takes you across a bridge parallel to the span of turbine outfalls that this plant seems so breathtaking. Or perhaps it's AlCan's massive aluminum plant next door, or possibly the tunnel that takes you under the river, just beyond. And then there are the Beauharnois locks. So much is happening here, and all on so grand a scale, it is impossible to imagine what is going on below the flow of the river.

A young woman guide at the Beauharnois visitor center (open, unlike the visitor center at the Moses–Saunders plant at Cornwall, which we will find has been closed to the public since September 11, 2001), explains to us the significance of the plant in Quebéc's history.

> Québec got a late start. We were like a colony, a reserve. We had nothing up through the DePlessis government which told women to stay home and have twenty or thirty babies and sold our only resource, iron, to a U.S. company for one cent per one ton.
>
> When the Québec government completed and nationalized this plant in the 1960s, it was our own power for our own people, the beginning of a new, free Québec. Now in Québec everyone has affordable power. And so we also have a strong social democracy. Our health care and our higher education systems, for example—everyone can go to college if they want to—are among the best in the world.

We had come prepared with questions: *How does this plant affect the river? What about the changing water levels? How does the operation affect the Atlantic salmon? The American eel?* But we are temporarily speechless before the history, the great project of Québec's energy independence, economic progress, and social democracy as she tells it. We leave wondering just how to insert river ecology into that compelling equation.

INTERLUDE

Second Voyage

AUGUST 12, 2006. Maureen and I leave homeport, Buck Pond State Park in the northern Adirondacks, on our second quest for the fabulous kingdom of the Haute-Gaspésie.

We break camp, stop in for a last farewell to the Faddens at the Six Nations Museum across the road, and drive to Hochelega where we find Highway 20, the express route, flowing all the to the City of Rimouski, which we reach by nightfall. We eat at Rimouski harbor—a dinner of steamed cod, "morou," fresh from the estuary.

From Rimouski we continue east on Route 132, leaving early Sunday morning to reach the Parc de la Gaspésie in time to set up camp that evening. Route 132 is the most beautiful road it is possible to see, following the south shore of the river through *cap et baie*—each bay with its little village and church nestled at the foot of the rising Appalachian massif. The landscape simplifies, openly revealing its natural and cultural history. Like apparently every other tourist heading east, we are arrested at Sainte-Flavie by a long procession of stone pilgrims emerging from the river and gathering at the roadside. They are fully present to us now at low tide. Marcel Gagnon's *Le Grand Rassemblement*, we learn in the vastness of his adjoining studio, restaurant, and gift shop, includes over a hundred life-size sculptures of these buttoned and buckled colonials—another version, perhaps, of *je me souviens,* with the tourist stationed in the native point of view.

Descending along one arm of the bay into Cap-Chat, we see the windmills of Le Nordais on the headland opposite. With seventy-five horizontal-axis wind generators plus Éole, the world's tallest vertical-axis turbine, Le Nordais is one of the largest wind parks in North America—capable of supplying 10,000 Québec homes with all their

10.1. ÉOLE, CAP-CHAT. "THE HIGHEST VERTICAL AXIS WIND TURBINE IN THE WORLD."

electricity needs. The parking lot is full of visitors from around the world awaiting the next guided tour.

At St. Anne du Mont we turn south into the Parc national de la Gaspésie, our base camp for the next week. From here we will explore the two mountain ranges that make up the Gaspé: the 600 million-year-old Gaspé mountains and the 160-million-year-old McGerrigles. Each marks a different era of land uplift as continental plates collided. Together they make up the North American end of the Appalachian Mountains—a chain, long since broken by continental drift, that extends across the Atlantic Ocean and up the west coast of Norway.

10.2. THE LAND HOLDS UP SIGNS

In the Parc de la Gaspé we observe more of native ways. To climb Mont Jacques Cartier, the second highest peak in the park, you must buy a ticket and be taken by bus to the trailhead in a remote section of the park. On the bus, you receive a lecture on the flora and fauna, and especially on how to behave near the endangered caribou, the only herd left south of the river. The population is in fact dwindling so fast that its numbers on the trail signs have been replaced year to year by hand: ~~250~~, ~~200~~, 160 animals. We see several caribou grazing on the summit, far outnumbered by the procession of several hundred hikers strung along behind and before us on the stony path.

On a windy day near the end of our journey we finally arrive at the seaside city of Gaspé on the Gulf of St Lawrence, where we seek out the Musée du Jacques Cartier to learn Québec's official version of the story of its birth. Here we find displays of artifacts and a video documentary on Cartier's life that credits him with first establishing French relations with the Indians, "though sometimes crudely, to be sure." A traveling exhibit, entitled "The Making of a Hero," provides a more illuminating *histoire*. It tells how Cartier died in poverty and was left in obscurity for 300 years until the Québec nationalist movement recreated him—beginning with a conjured French face on a postage stamp and the first of hundreds of ceremonials enacting his erection of the cross at the entrance to Gaspé Harbor. Outside the museum stands a replica of the 30-foot cross.

We buy supplies at a grocery in Jacques Cartier shopping mall on Jacques Cartier Boulevard and head back upriver to our camp. The great river-estuary flows down on our right, its far shore too distant to be seen. Mountain strata bend skyward on the left. The tide is in, the sun is low, the land holds up signs revealing the physical and cultural collisions that have shaped it.

TEN

LEOPOLD REVISITED

A thing is right when it tends to preserve the integrity, stability and beauty of the biotic community. It is wrong when it tends otherwise.

—Aldo Leopold

THE DEAD AND BURNING Great Lakes waters of the 1960s helped pressure President Nixon to sign the 1970 National Environmental Policy Act, creating a process for public intervention in proposed actions that could significantly degrade the environment. In 1975, New York passed its state version, the State Environmental Quality Review Act (SEQRA), which further defined "significant environmental impact" in terms of the size of a project's footprint and whether it would require changes in existing permits or land use regulations. But SEQRA has turned out to be a weak first line of defense for our lakes and rivers. Local governments, often acting as lead agencies in SEQRA reviews, generally pass projects right through the first screening with a quick "Neg Dec" (negative declaration) as to their significance. Relatively few plans receive the full environmental impact assessment that would help decide how to reduce or avoid damages to "the integrity, stability and beauty of the biotic community." Without those reviews, our collective knowledge of the health of our local biotic community, including its human members, is diminished. As buildings, roads, parking lots, and strip malls further alter or efface natural systems, the capacity to make "right" decisions going forward is even further diminished.

Aldo Leopold's conservation ethic requires a sustained effort in the opposite direction. It requires "a biotic view of the land," as he titles one of his papers. This view, now a staple at least in elementary school science curricula, understands life on earth as a fountain of energy powered by the sun and grounded in the soil and water. Food chains are living channels that conduct the energy upward; death and decay return it to the soil. "The upward flow of energy depends on the complex structure of the plant and animal community, much as the upward flow of sap in a tree depends on its complex cellular organization." The interdependence of soil, water, plants, and animals within this energy circuit means that the "economic parts" cannot function without the "uneconomic parts." Leopold further breaks it down into these three basic ideas:

1. That land is not merely soil.
2. That the native plants and animals kept the energy circuit open; others may or may not.
3. That man-made changes are of a different order than evolutionary changes, and have effects more comprehensive than is intended or foreseen.[1]

In light of these concepts, changes to the land and water that will require large and continuous inputs of human energy to sustain them are neither ethically right nor economical. They are likely to be as destructive over the long term in direct proportion to how large (or "violent," to use Leopold's word) they are. The 10,000-year maintenance schedule for radioactive wastes buried at the West Valley site is one example of the scale of unintended effects that can be caused by man-made changes decided in relative ignorance of the land and water as the foundation of a living energy circuit.

PERHAPS FOR THE FIRST TIME in human history, two world powers, Canada and the United States, committed to a purpose very much in keeping with Leopold's conservation ethic when they amended the Great Lakes Water Quality Agreement in 1978.

The purpose of the Parties is to restore and maintain the chemical, physical, and biological integrity of the waters of the

Great Lakes Basin Ecosystem. In order to achieve this purpose, the Parties agree to make a maximum effort to develop programs, practices and technology necessary for a better understanding of the Great Lakes Basin Ecosystem and to eliminate or reduce to the maximum extent practicable the discharge of pollutants into the Great Lakes System.[2]

In December 2005, Great Lakes regional leaders agreed to two more collaborations that begin to provide the regulatory structures and financial supports to achieve this purpose. The first of these, the *Great Lakes Water Resources Compact*[3] signed in principle by the governors of all eight Great Lakes states and the premiers of Ontario and Québec, is designed to protect the region from projects that would divert, export, or otherwise use large amounts of water. Passed by Congress and signed into U.S. law in 2008, the compact amends earlier agreements governing Great Lakes water diversions in three important ways. It is binding, it sets strict limits on the amount of water that could be sent out of the basin, and it regulates in-basin water use, setting thresholds for consumption based on ecosystem protection. "The Parties agree that *the protection of the Great Lakes-St. Lawrence River Basin Ecosystem* shall be the overarching principle for reviewing proposals." Thus, the compact inserts the "uneconomic part" of maintaining the Great Lakes biotic energy circuit into the usual economic equations governing water use.

Also in December 2005, a collaboration of Great Lakes governors, mayors, agency heads, tribal leaders, environmental groups, and industry representatives in the United States released a *Strategy to Restore and Protect the Great Lakes*[4]—a detailed set of science-based recommendations directed toward eliminating pollution and restoring ecosystems. The fifty-page strategy with its five-hundred-page appendix reflects both the consensus-building and fine-tuning work of its diverse writers. As a bill calling for a federal investment of $26 billion in the Great Lakes and their tributary rivers, the strategy still awaits Congressional action. However, the process of its creation gave rise to a regional movement, the Healing Our Waters coalition, dedicated to implementing the strategy's objectives.

Although, as of this writing, only the Great Lakes Compact has been fully authorized, both of these broad-based initiatives will now help shape the culture of decision-making relative to Great Lakes waters. How are they relevant to the rivers we have just explored? How do they relate to the key ideas behind Leopold's conservation ethic?

LAND IS NOT MERELY SOIL

IN TERMS OF THE amount of funding required—about $15 billion—the top goal of the Great Lakes Strategy is to fix the problem of sewage overflows. "By 2020 or sooner where possible, eliminate inputs of untreated or inadequately treated human and industrial waste to Great Lakes basin waters from municipal wastewater treatment systems." Over one hundred basin communities, including the city of Buffalo are in basic violation of the Clean Water Act due to overflows of untreated sewage directly into tributaries like Scajaquada Creek and the Buffalo River. Sewer authorities ascribe the problem to lack of funding for system upgrades, yet the options they have offered taxpayers almost always involve expensive engineering to build greater retention capacity. In Buffalo, the "best option" proposed is a "deep tunnel" underground storage system costing $1 billion. Multiply that by a hundred other cities across the basin with inadequate wastewater treatment and we might well be wondering if $15 billion is anywhere near the amount we really need.

However, if the history of Scajaquada Creek has taught us anything, it is that more diversion of its natural flow, even if the city could raise the money for the most expensive deep tunnel project, will lead to more problems down the line. We can learn from the experience of other Great Lake cities as well. In Milwaukee, a $716-million, 20-mile-long underground sewage storage tunnel has not only failed to eliminate overflows into the city's waterways but also now pollutes groundwater in some areas of the district.

The strategy's approach to sewage overflows recognizes that "land is not merely soil," that undeveloped permeable land, for example, has high ecosystem and economic value in its capacity to hold water. It proposes a federal grant program rewarding communities whose overflow elimination plans incorporate the tactic of reducing the volume of stormwater going into the wastewater collection system—as opposed to building bigger systems. In the case of Scajaquada Creek, this would require coordinated planning with upstream suburbs in the sewershed to protect and restore wetlands, floodplains, and other "green infrastructure" that slow the movement of stormwater, ensuring maximum absorption on the land where it falls. An additional benefit is smarter growth—curbing sprawl by incorporating the hydrologic value of undeveloped land in municipal land use management planning. In most of our communities, this link between wastewater system engineers and land use planners has yet to be made. Federal criteria selecting for projects with green infrastructure components would encourage that conversation to begin.

Land is also riverbeds supporting an aquatic food chain flowing up through the fish and those who consume them. The strategy sets a goal of cleaning up sediments in the Great Lakes' most industrially polluted rivers and harbors by 2020. In many places, like the Buffalo River, we know where the toxic hotspots are, based on sampling and modeling in relation to contaminant sources and transport patterns. There is a window of opportunity to remove, treat, and, where necessary, secure them out of reach of living communities before they are irretrievably flushed out into the lakes.

NATIVE SPECIES KEEP THE ENERGY CIRCUIT OPEN

RECALL HERE Leopold's second premise in the model for healthy biotic communities: "That the native plants and animals kept the energy circuit open; others may or may not." This is not a nativist bias. It respects a stability arrived at only through generations of coevolution.

In the last weeks of November 2007, hundreds of migrating loons died at the eastern end of Lake Erie from another outbreak of avian botulism. The toxic bacteria *Clostridium botulinum* has resided naturally in the Great Lakes for decades with small effect on wildlife. However, since 1999, we have lost hundreds of thousands of fish and fish-eating birds—including gulls, loons, diving ducks, and shorebirds—to drowning from paralysis caused by ingestion of the botulinum bacteria. Based on the stomach contents of dead birds, it appears that two relatively new nonnative species—the quagga mussel cousin of the zebra mussel and the round goby, a small mussel-eating fish—are responsible for mobilizing the bacteria into the food chain. Tracing them back to their origins in places like the Caspian Sea, scientists believe that these species and many others are introduced through ballast water discharges from foreign ships entering the Great Lakes via the St. Lawrence Seaway.

The Great Lakes Strategy recommends stronger National Aquatic Invasive Species legislation requiring shipboard ballast water treatment for all oceangoing cargo vessels. It also proposes "back-up approaches," including moving cargo from large oceangoing vessels to smaller Great Lakes carriers prior to entry into the system. Such an approach would not only close a major avenue of exotic species introductions, it would remove the need to further pursue schemes to enlarge the St. Lawrence Seaway and navigation channel to accommodate supersized container ships. Given the fact that containers account for less than 1 percent of freight tonnage on the seaway, the time may be ripe for exploring the cargo transfer approach as one that could benefit both the ecosystem and the regional shipping economy.

The strategy also calls for reevaluation of the region's canal systems as vectors for new nonnative aquatic species, and for closure or creation of barriers on canals where the threat exists. Ideally, the New York State Thruway Authority will reassess its annual multi-million dollar investment in the purely recreational Erie Canal in light of its continuing potential as an invasive species vector and its impacts on the Oswego River, Montezuma Swamp, and other river and wetland ecosystems across the state.

MAN-MADE CHANGES HAVE UNINTENDED COMPREHENSIVE EFFECTS

THE MAGNITUDE of what we don't know concerning the true ecosystem costs of large-scale hydropower diversions looms ever larger in the face of projected increases in energy demand and decreases in Great Lakes water levels caused by climate change. We do know that "natural flow regimes" are important to healthy rivers and that, in the case of

Niagara, power plant operations interrupt natural flows and water levels in the river and its tributaries on a daily basis, taking a toll on aquatic communities and the birds and other wildlife that depend on them.

The *Great Lakes Compact* calls for increased research on the ecological benefits of naturally running rivers, for stronger laws governing water diversions even where the water is returned downstream, and for regional water conservation policies and programs. The burden of proof is on the potential user to demonstrate that any major taking of water will not harm the ecosystem. Such an approach would greatly benefit the Niagara River, especially if supported by federal and state energy programs and incentives that decrease our electricity use and consequent demand on the river.

In the larger picture, New York State's energy portfolio is dangerously reliant on large-scale man-made alterations of the land whose unintended damages are potentially equally far-reaching. At this writing, less than 4 percent of the electricity produced in the state comes from low-impact renewable sources like solar, wind, and biomass. Nuclear and coal-fired power plants account for about 47 percent, oil and natural gas for another 34 percent, and mega-hydropower from the two plants on the Niagara and St. Lawrence Rivers for the remaining 15 percent. Promises of "clean coal" and "a new Manhattan Project" of nuclear power development may actually increase the amounts of fossil fuels mined and burned—despite the limited reserves, unsustainable mining practices, and end-of-the-pipe lessons we have seen proven in our surface and groundwaters.

Sixteen nuclear reactors reside on Lake Ontario's Canadian and U.S. shores, perpetuating our region's unsolved problem of radioactive waste and threatening catastrophe if a major malfunction at any one facility occurs. Four of these are in New York State: the Ginna pressurized water reactor near Rochester, and three boiling water reactors just east of the City of Oswego—Fitzpatrick and Nine Mile Point Units One and Two. Nine Mile One, completed in 1969, is among the oldest nuclear plants in the country, and has had the cracks in its core shrouds (structures that enclose the fuel rods and assure coolant flow though the core) to show it. Nevertheless, in October 2006, the Nuclear Regulatory Commission extended the operating licenses for Nine Mile One and Two for an additional twenty years—to 2029 and 2046, respectively. It appears that the problems plaguing the West Valley site have failed to impress our federal and state energy regulators as a cautionary tale.

Many Great Lakes states are in the process of adopting standards of at least 20 percent energy generation from renewable sources by 2020. However, as we have learned in New York, we need a national sustainable energy policy to truly protect the biotic energy circuit currently being sacrificed to burning fossil fuels and large-scale river diversions.

INTELLIGENT CONSUMPTION

FINALLY, although it is not specifically included in either the strategy or the compact, I want to introduce Leopold's term "intelligent consumption" by way of revisiting the salt mine collapse in the Genesee Valley. Leopold coined the phrase in 1928 to discuss how the home building industry could influence forest management and to address the individual as opposed to the government role in promoting the land ethic.[5]

Because of advocates like the Canadian Auto Workers (CAW) union, "clean production" is perhaps the more comprehensive term with greater name recognition in the Great Lakes region. Clean production, which includes the idea of intelligent consumption, embraces a circular or nonlinear use of Earth's materials. "It requires thinking of the production of goods as part of a life cycle that includes the extraction and processing of raw materials, product design, consumption, and disposal in which the product eventually becomes raw materials."[6] Labor unions like the CAW support clean production policies not just to protect the environment, but also to protect jobs in a global marketplace that increasingly demands products like cars to be designed to meet end-of-life recycling requirements. Sweden, Germany, and other European nations require "extended producer responsibility" of their automobile and appliance manufacturers, who must take back these products at the end of their lives and therefore design them to be recyclable.

A clean production approach might have averted the undermining of Little Beard's section of the Genesee Valley by fully assessing the need for salt extraction in the first place, given the environmental risks that come with both mining and use. The Canadian Environmental

Protection Act lists road salt as a toxic substance because of its potential to pollute groundwater and kill vegetation. Requiring highway departments to do full cost accounting, including the costs of replacing roadside trees or treating local streams and groundwater, might make the more environmentally benign alternatives to salt now available more attractive.

The "intelligent consumption" part of the clean production cycle is useful for thinking about the afterlife of the salt mine, specifically the plan to dispose of municipal garbage incinerator ash in the mined-out cavities. This scenario not only would have risked future groundwater contamination from mercury, dioxin, and other toxins concentrated in the ash, but also would have enabled the most linear and wasteful use of resources imaginable. In 2004, over 50 percent (about 310,000 tons) of Buffalo and Erie County's garbage was incinerated, and the ash disposed of in a Niagara County hazardous waste landfill. In 2007, the city of Buffalo reported a garbage recycling rate of only 6.5 percent, compared to a national average for cities of about 30 percent, with cities like Toronto and Guelph recycling well over 50 percent of their municipal waste.

These facts represent a failure of our governments to set and meet strong requirements for reducing waste. But they also challenge every one of us, as individuals, to reduce our consumption and to choose the products we do buy in terms of their "cradle-to-grave" costs to our living land and waters. "Who is the land?" Leopold asks. "We are, but no less than the meanest flower that blows."[7]

READING RIVERS is a complicated business. You must know your toxicology, your hydrology, your biology, your chemistry, your physics, and your law. You should be aware of when the sewers kick in, where the wastes are buried, what the ships could be carrying in their ballast waters. You must think about the places, processes, and materials used in manufacturing and destroying the products you consume and throw away.

I am tempted at this point to start another list—a "what you can do" list that would probably span a range similar to Theo Colborn's in her conclusion to *Our Stolen Future*. Her final recommendations begin with "Know your water" and end with "Redesign the manufacture and use of chemicals."[8] Mine might begin with "Follow your river to its source" and end with "Buy less, buy local, buy as if you were account-able for the life cycle of the product" (which we are). But I'd rather recount my most recent visit to Baraboo, Wisconsin, where Leopold had a shack and did much of the fieldwork that informed the last decade of his writing.

IT IS A BRIGHT DECEMBER MORNING, thermometer hovering at 0 degrees Fahrenheit, 2 feet of thinly crusted snow on the ground. County Highway T leads out of the picturesque little village of Bara-boo, past dairy farms on one side of the road facing brand new half-acre-lot subdivisions on the other. Some homes are already occupied, though the land around them is still raw and torn. Neil and I cannot help thinking that, though Wisconsin is America's Dairy State, the sub-divisions are winning. After 10 minutes, we turn and travel another 10 through pure dairyland with scatterings of black angus and then woods. The Wisconsin River shimmers behind its forested floodplain on the left. The Wisconsin is, of course, not part of our Great Lakes ecosystem; it drains south to the Mississippi. Along with the Fox River connecting the two watersheds, it was once a critical part of the water route to the Gulf of Mexico and of the fur trade route east to Atlantic ports. The Wisconsin was and is also part of a great midwestern north–south wildlife corridor still used today by sandhill cranes, elk, and the occa-sional wolf.

We turn again onto a tiny "Rural Road" through a forest of black oak and pines. Now we are on the land of the Leopold Legacy Center, once a dust bowl farm that Leopold purchased in 1935 "for its lack of goodness and its lack of highway." Here he, his wife Estella, and their five children lived part time between 1935 and 1948, when Leopold died of a heart attack fighting a grass fire. His day job was teaching wildlife ecology at the University of Wisconsin in Madison, about an hour south from here. This farm was his workshop for restoring health to an ailing piece of land—a place where the family eventually planted 40,000 trees. It is now the core of some 11,000 acres of public and pri-vate land spanning miles of Wisconsin River floodplain and adjacent upland dedicated to wildlife conservation.

We pass a tiny, boarded-up cabin, round a bend, and arrive at the Aldo Leopold Legacy Center—a complex of classrooms, meeting rooms, archives, and library designed after Leopold's conservation ethic. The buildings and much of the furniture are made of pine, oak, cherry, and red maple harvested to thin and strengthen the surrounding forest. Solar panels help heat the center, but the primary means of heating and cooling is a geothermal radiant floor system tapped into the earth's 55-degree Fahrenheit constant temperature through pipes and wells beneath the ground. Over the course of a year, the Legacy Center produces more energy than it consumes.

After chatting with one of the center's ecologists, Steve Swenson, who describes how Leopold and family skied in to their shack in the winter using two pairs of skis (two Leopolds in, one out carrying the extra skis to the next family member waiting up at the road), we head back to the shack itself. We follow deer tracks through the crusty snow, noting all the deer-pruned dogwood circling the little weathered house, wondering how a family of seven could have possibly all fit in. Behind it the land steps down a few feet to floodplain level and to the Wisconsin River flowing somewhere back there, screened by a forest of winter trees. I try to see what Leopold saw. The snow is full of all kinds of tracks, including those of some kind of wide-bellied animal with a skinny tail. Our pants and scarves and gloves are studded with seeds from the tangle of dried grasses and shrubs poking up through the snow. We hear chittering sounds and a bald eagle flies into view, landing on the branch of a tree about 100 feet ahead to observe us. She is the third unexpected bald eagle I have seen this year. We crunch back to the road where a red-headed woodpecker is hammering away at a dead pine, probably planted there by Aldo or Estella.

NOTES

INTRODUCTION

1. Aldo Leopold, "The Land Ethic," in *A Sand County Almanac and Sketches Here and There* (London: Oxford University Press, 1949), 214.

2. "Haudenosaunee," meaning "People of the Longhouse," is the aboriginal name for the six nations —Seneca, Tuscarora, Cayuga, Oneida, Onondaga, and Mohawk—of the Iroquois Confederacy.

1. THE GLOBAL CONTEXT

1. United Nations World Water Assessment Programme, *World Water Development Reports 1 and 2* (Paris and New York: UNESCO and Berghahn Books, 2003 and 2006), www.unesco.org/water/wwap.

2. See, for example, J. A. Stafford and J. V. Ward, "An Ecosystem Perspective of Alluvial Rivers" in *Journal of the American Benthological Society*, 1993, vol. 12, 48–60.

3. Masaru Emoto, *Messages from Water*, Tokyo video productions. Also www.hadousa.com.

4. International Joint Commission United States and Canada, *Revised Great Lakes Water Quality Agreement of 1978* (Washington, DC, and Ottawa: IJC, Reprint February 1994), 4.

5. International Joint Commission, *Sixth Biennial Report on Great Lakes Water Quality* (Washington, DC, Ottawa, and Windsor: IJC, 1992), 15–17. The IJC consists of six commissioners (three appointed by the head of each country) and advisory boards, including a Great Lakes Science and a Great Lakes Water Quality Advisory Board.

6. Theo Colborn, Dianne Dumanoski, and John Peterson Myers, *Our Stolen Future* (New York: Penguin Books, 1997).

7. Environmental Defence and Canadian Environmental Law Association, *Partners in Pollution: An Assessment of Continuing Canadian and United States Contributions to Great Lakes Pollution* (Toronto: CELA, 2006), www.cela.ca/.

8. U.S. Environment Protection Agency and Environment Canada, *State of the Great Lakes 2007, Highlights Report*, 3, www.epa.gov/glnpo/solec/sogl2007.

9. Michael Williams, *Citizens Speak* (Buffalo: Great Lakes United, 1999), 12.

10. Leopold, "The Land Ethic" in *A Sand County Almanac and Sketches Here and There*, 224–25.

2. WHAT IS NIAGARA?

1. Since 1994, when Canada, the United States, and Mexico signed NAFTA or the North American Free Trade Agreement, the Peace Bridge over the Niagara River has become a major truck crossing.

2. Orasmus H. Marshall, "The Niagara Frontier," *Publications of the Buffalo Historical Society*, Volume II (Buffalo: Bigelow Brothers, 1880). Marshall is the source for all interpretations of Indian names used in this book unless otherwise indicated.

3. John Mohawk, prologue to Paul A. W. Wallace, *The White Roots of Peace* (Saranac Lake: Chauncy Press, 1986), xvi.

4. Joanne Shenandoah and Douglas M. George, *Skywoman: Legends of the Iroquois* (Santa Fe: Clear Light Publishers, 1998), 100.

5. See, for example, Donald A. Grinde Jr. and Bruce E. Johansen, *Exemplar of Liberty: Native America and the Evolution of Democracy* (Los Angeles: University of California Press, 1991).

6. L. Hennepin, *New Discovery of a Vast Country in America* (London: M. Bentley, 1698), 29.

7. Laurence M. Hauptman, *The Iroquois Struggle for Survival* (Syracuse: Syracuse University Press, 1986).

8. See, for example, Stantec Consulting Services, Inc., *Effect of Water Level and Flow Fluctuations on Aquatic and Terrestrial Habitat* (Albany: NY Power Authority, 2004).

9. Tom DeSantis, *Niagara's Parks: International Stewardship from an Ecological Perspective*, unpublished master's thesis (Buffalo: School of Architecture and Planning, SUNY Buffalo, 1996).

10. Robert Borgatti and Paul Lamont, *Fading in the Mist*, a video documentary of the Free Niagara Movement, 1996.

11. See "The International Niagara Peace Park" at www.urbandesignproject.ap.buffalo.edu. For more on the Niagara Heritage Partnership, see www.niagaraheritage.org. For more on the Niagara Escarpment Biosphere

Reserve, see www.escarpment.org. For more on the Niagara Peace Park, see Kerry Mitchell, *Pathway to Peace: What Heritage Based Collaboration Offers the Cross-Border Niagara Region*, 2004, available on the first two Web sites.

3. SCAJAQUADA: PORTRAIT OF AN URBAN CREEK

1. Moses Shongo, "Indian Collection 1788–1955" Box 1, Folder 15, no date. Buffalo Historical Society research library. Handwritten by Shongo on BHS letterhead, apparently in response to a series of questions about local place names. Shongo was the grandfather of Twylah Hurd Nitsch. He died in the early 1920s.

2. Hennepin, *New Discovery of a Vast Country in America*, 66–78.

3. New York State Department of Environmental Conservation, *Contaminants in Young-of-Year Fish from Selected Lake Ontario Tributaries* (Albany: NYS DEC, December 1996).

4. Margaret Fess, "Thousand Cross Main St. Bridge and Never Know It," *Buffalo Courier Express*, January 20, 1952, 16B.

5. Ibid.

6. G. Williams Beardslee, "The 1832 Cholera Epidemic in New York State: 19th Century Responses to *Cholerae Vibrio*," http://earlyamerica.com/review/2000_fall/1832_cholera.html.

7. League of Women Voters, "Education Campaign on Urban Sprawl," www.lwvbn.org/sprawl/.

8. See Judy L. Meyer et al., *Where Rivers Are Born: The Scientific Imperative for Defending Small Streams and Watersheds* (Athens, GA: American Rivers and Sierra Club, 2003) for a discussion of the ecosystem functions of springs and headwaters.

9. Arthur C. Parker, *The Life of General Ely S. Parker*, Editorial Notes (Buffalo: Buffalo Historical Society, 1919), 313–17.

4. BUFFALO RIVER ABANDONED

1. K. N. Irvine et al., *Assessment of Potential Aquatic Habitat Restoration Sites in the Buffalo River Area of Concern* (Buffalo, Buffalo State SUNY, October 2005). These findings, based on a 2004 survey of the AOC, found either no significant change or "possibly some reversal in biotic recovery" compared to studies done in the early 1990s.

2. See, for example, William Cronon, *Changes in the Land: Indians, Colonists, and the Ecology of New England* (New York: Farrar, Straus and Giroux, 1983), 82–107.

3. Frederick Houghton, "History of the Buffalo Creek Reservation," in *Buffalo Historical Society Publications*, Volume XXIV (Buffalo: Buffalo Historical Society, 1920), 18–19.

4. Walter McCausland, "The People of Seneca Indian Park," in *Niagara Frontier*, Winter 1963, Vol. 9, No. 4, 82–83.

5. James Wilson, *The Earth Shall Weep: A History of Native America* (New York: Atlantic Monthly Press, 1998), 111.

6. Marshall, "The Niagara Frontier," 423.

7. Gilbert J. Pedersen, "Early Title to Indian Reservations in Western New York," *Niagara Frontier*, 1956–1957, Vol. 3, 7.

8. Reyner Banham et al., *Buffalo Architecture: A Guide* (Cambridge: MIT Press, 1982), 12.

9. David E. Sauer, *An Environmental History of the Buffalo River* (Buffalo: Buffalo Color Corporation, 1979), 17.

10. From "Concerns and Requests of the Seneca-Babcock Good Neighbor Committee," presented to the Buffalo Common Council, July 19, 1994.

11. From a personal interview with Stan Spisiak, August 23, 1993.

12. The Waterkeeper Alliance, whose president is Robert F. Kennedy Jr., is "a grassroots advocacy organization dedicated to preserving and protecting *your water* from polluters." See www.waterkeeper.org.

5. GENESEE TORTURE TREE:
REREADING LITTLE BEARD'S SIGNS

1. Herman Leroy Fairchild, *Geologic Story of the Genesee Valley and Western New York* (Rochester, NY: published by the author, 1928).

2. John C. Fitzpatrick, ed., "Instructions to Major General John Sullivan," *The Writings of George Washington*, Vol. 15 (Washington, DC: U.S. Government Printing Office, 1936), 191.

3. See, for example, Thomas S. Abler, *Chainbreaker: The Revolutionary War Memoirs of Governor Blacksnake* (Lincoln: University of Nebraska Press, 1989), 115.

4. James E. Sever, ed., *A Narrative of the Life of Mrs. Mary Jemison* (Syracuse: Syracuse University Press, 1990), 57.

5. Jeanette Marvin, "Finding a Fault at Akzo Nobel's New Mine," *Country Folks West*, November 27, 1995, 4.

6. See, for example, Bryan G. Norton, *Sustainability: A Philosophy of Adaptive Ecosystem Management* (Chicago: University of Chicago Press, 2005).

7. Wes Jackson, quoting a personal letter from Wendell Berry in "Toward an Ignorance-based Worldview," in *The Land Report* (Salinas, KS: The Land Institute, Spring 2005, No. 81), 14–16, www.landinstitute.org

6. ZOAR VALLEY GENESIS

1. U.S. Environmental Protection Agency, *New Index of Environmental Condition for Coastal Watersheds in the Great Lakes Basin* (Washington, DC: EPA Office of Research and Development, 2005); and David M.Hunt et al., *Lake Erie Gorges: Biodiversity Inventory and Landscape Integrity Analysis* (Albany: New York Natural Heritage Program, October 2002).

2. Genesis 13: 9–10, *The Oxford Annotated Bible with the Apocrypha*, ed. Herbert May and Bruce Metzger (New York: Oxford University Press, 1962).

3. Eber Russell, "On the Death of Arthur Parker," Russell Papers, from the collection of Patterson Library, Westfield, NY, #2, 1.

4. Arthur C. Parker, *Seneca Myths and Folk Tales* (Lincoln: University of Nebraska Press, 1989), 70–71.

5. Jeremiah Curtin, *Seneca Myths and Legends* (New York: E. P. Dutton, 1923), 6–7.

6. Irving H. Tesmer, *Geology of Cattaraugus County* (Buffalo: Buffalo Society of Natural Sciences Bulletin, Vol. 27, 1975), 14.

7. Richard S. Laub, ed., *The Hiscock Site: Late Pleistocene and Early Holocene Paleoecology and Archaeology of Western New York State* (Buffalo: Buffalo Society of Natural Sciences Bulletin, Vol. 37, 2003).

8. Carol Mongerson, *West Valley Nuclear Waste, A Citizen's View* (unpublished manuscript, copyright December 2002), 5.

9. Russell, "Manuscript for Pioneer Map between left border and Taylor Hollow Road," Russell Papers, #25, 6.

10. Raymond C. Vaughan et al., *Geology Reports of the Coalition on West Valley Nuclear Wastes* (East Concord, NY: Coalition on West Valley Nuclear Wastes, 1994).

11. Russell Papers, #23, 1.

12. Paul A. W. Wallace, *The White Roots of Peace*, with prologue by John Mohawk (Saranac Lake: Chauncy Press, 1986), xix.

7. HIGH PEAKS, CLOUD LAKES

1. Michael G. DiNunzio, *Adirondack Wildguide: A Natural History of the Adirondack Park* (Keene Valley, NY: Adirondack Nature Conservancy, 1984), 17–21.

2. The film is based on B. Traven's book, *The Treasure of the Sierra Madre* (New York: Noonday Press, 1935), from which I have taken the precise quote.

3. Dennis Aprill, ed., *Good Fishing in the Adirondacks* (Woodstock, NY: Backcountry Publications, 1999), 14–16.

4. Ray Fadden, or "Tahenetorens," is succeeded at the Six Nations Museum by his son John and grandsons David and Donald, all of whom continue to share Mohawk stories and traditions through painting, drawing, and story-telling. For a bibliography of some of their work, go to http://tuscaroras.com/graydeer/pages/sixnamus.htm.

5. Eliot Spitzer, *Submission to the Commission on Environmental Cooperation to Develop a Record on Ontario Power Generation's Failure to Enforce Environmental Laws,* May 1, 2003.

6. John Slade, *Acid Rain, Acid Snow* (New York: Woodgate International, 2000), 4–5.

7. Anne LaBastille, "Death from the Sky" from *Beyond Black Bear Lake* (New York: W.W. Norton, 1987).

8. The Adirondack Council is a nonprofit organization dedicated to ensuring the ecological integrity and wild character of the Adirondack Park. Their testimony on S.131, "The Clear Skies Act of 2005," was read by executive director Brian Houseal on February 2, 2005.

9. Charles Driscoll et al., *Acid Rain Revisited: Advances in Scientific Understanding Since the Passage of the 1970 and 1990 Clean Air Act Amendments* (Hanover, NH: Hubbard Brook Research Foundation, Science Links Publication, Vol. 1, No. 1), 21.

10. Alice Outwater, *Water: A Natural History* (New York: Basic Books, 1996), 21.

8. OSWEGO, ONONDAGA, AND THE POLITICS OF LISTING

1. See Erhard Rostlund, *Freshwater Fish and Fishing in Native North America* (Berkeley: University of California Press, 1952), for historical maps of native fish ranges.

2. J. M. Casselman et al., "Status of the Upper St. Lawrence River and Lake Ontario American Eel Stock—1996," pp. 106–20. In R. H. Peterson, ed.,

Proceedings of Eel Workshop, January 13–14 1997, Canadian Technical Report of Fisheries and Aquatic Sciences, No. 2196 (St. Andrews, NB, Fisheries and Oceans, Canada, 1997).

3. See the "Lake Ontario Committee" section of the Great Lakes Fishery Commission's Web site, www.glfc.org, for information on the American eel, including a white paper on the reasons for decline of the Lake Ontario–St. Lawrence River substock.

4. Outwater, *Water: A Natural History*, 113.

5. New York Power Authority, "Final Report: Historic Presence and Current Status of Atlantic Salmon in the St. Lawrence River and Lake Ontario," 2004, public record.

6. New York State Canal Corporation, *A Report on the Future of New York State Canals* (December 2005, Appendix 1), 103. See www.canals.state.ny.us.

7. U.S. Fish and Wildlife Service, *2006 National Survey of Fishing, Hunting and Wildlife-Associated Recreation* (Washington, DC, USFWS, November 2007).

8. New York State Department of Environmental Conservation, "Oswego River RAP: Stage 3—Delisting," (Albany: NYSDEC, May 2002), 21.

9. Wallace, *The White Roots of Peace*, 15. (Referenced hereafter as WRP, page number.)

10. Edward Michalenko, ed., *The State of Onondaga Lake* (Syracuse: Onondaga Lake Cleanup Corp., 2001).

11. Status Consulting, Inc., "Technical Analysis of Baseline Ecological Risk Assessment and Proposed Remedial Action Plan for Mercury in Onondaga Lake" (Nedrow, NY: The Onondaga Nation, June 2005), S 2–3.

9. LE FLEUVE

1. At IJC biennial public meetings held since 1983 in the Great Lakes region, both Québec and First Nations advocacy groups have gone on record demanding formal inclusion as parties to the Great Lakes Water Quality Agreement.

2. See U.S. Geological Survey, Great Lakes Science Center, "Zebra Mussels Cause Economic and Ecological Harm in the Great Lakes" at www.glsc.usgs.gov/-files/factsheets.

3. *The Voyages of Jacques Cartier*, trans. Henry Percival Biggar (Toronto: University of Toronto Press, 1993). (Referenced hereafter as C, page number.)

4. Pennsylvania Transportation Institute, *Analysis of the Great Lakes/St. Lawrence River Navigation System's Role in U.S. Ocean Container Trade* (University

Park: Pennsylvania State University, August 2003). See also the CBC website http://archives.cbc.ca/IDD-1-69-637/life-society/seaway for a Canadian analysis of seaway obsolescence.

5. Donald A. Grinde and Bruce Johansen, "Akwesasne's Toxic Turtles" from *Ecocide of Native America: Environmental Destruction of Indian Lands and People* (Santa Fe: Clear Light Publishers, 1995).

6. Haudenosaunee Environmental Task Force, *Words that Come Before All Else* (Akwesasne, Ontario: Native North American Travelling College, 1999), 39–40.

7. John Fiske, *New France and New England* (Boston: Houghton, Mifflin, 1902), 15.

8. See www.whales-online.net to read about and hear examples of the acoustic environments of belugas.

9. Theo Colborn et al., *Our Stolen Future*, 145–46.

10. See research by former IJC Commissioner Pierre Béland and others at www.whales-online.net.

11. William T. Vollman, *Fathers and Crows, Volume II of Seven Dreams: A Book of North American Landscapes* (New York: Viking, 1992), 312–13.

12. John Fiske, *New France and New England*, 42.

10. LAST WORD

1. Leopold, *A Sand County Almanac*, 218.

2. *The Great Lakes Water Quality Agreement*, Article II, 4.

3. Find the full text of the *Great Lakes Waters Resources Compact* (December 2005) on the Council of Great Lakes Governors' Web site www.cglg.org.

4. Great Lakes Regional Collaboration, *Strategy to Restore and Protect the Great Lakes* (December 2005), www.glrc.us.

5. Aldo Leopold, "The Home Builder Conserves" in *The River of the Mother of God and Other Essays by Aldo Leopold,* ed. Susan L. Flader and J. Baird Callicott (Madison: University of Wisconsin Press, 1991), 143.

6. See the Lowell Center for Sustainable Production Web site http://sustainableproduction.org. Colborn et al., *Our Stolen Future*, 226–27.

7. "The Role of Wildlife in a Liberal Education [1942]" in *The River of the Mother of God and Other Essays*, 303.

8. Theo Colbrn et al., *Our Stolen Future*, 212–30.

BIBLIOGRAPHY

Abler, Thomas S. *Chainbreaker: The Revolutionary War Memoirs of Governor Black-snake.* Lincoln: University of Nebraska Press, 1989.

Abrams, George H. J. *The Seneca People.* Phoenix: Indian Tribal Series, 1976.

Aprill, Dennis, editor. *Good Fishing in the Adirondacks.* Woodstock, NY: Back-country Publications, 1999.

Banham, Reyner et al. *Buffalo Architecture: A Guide.* Cambridge: MIT Press, 1982.

Beardslee, G. Williams. *The 1832 Cholera Epidemic in New York State: 19th Century Responses to* Cholerae Vibrio. http://earlyamerica.com/review/2000_fall/1832_cholera.html.

Berg, Peter. *Figures of Regulation.* San Francisco: Planet Drum Foundation, 1983.

Biggar, Henry Percival, translator. *The Voyages of Jacques Cartier.* Toronto: University of Toronto Press, 1993.

Borgatti, Robert, and Paul Lamont. *Fading in the Mist,* a video documentary of the Free Niagara Movement, 1996.

Botts, Lee, and Paul Muldoon. *The Great Lakes Water Quality Agreement: Its Past Successes and Uncertain Future.* Hanover: Dartmouth College, 1997.

Brant, Joseph. *Indian Collection,* Box 1, folder 2. Buffalo and Erie County Historical Museum.

Carmer, Carl. *Dark Trees to the Wind.* New York: William Sloane Associates, 1949.

Chandler, James E. "The Hiscock Site" in Center for the Study of the First Americans, Volume 16, Number 4. www.centerfirstamericans.com.

Colborn, Theo, Dianne Dumanoski, and John P. Myers. *Our Stolen Future.* New York: Penguin Books, 1997.

Cronon, William. *Changes in the Land: Indians, Colonists, and the Ecology of New England.* New York: Farrar, Straus and Giroux, 1983.

Curtin, Jeremiah. *Seneca Myths and Legends.* New York: E. P. Dutton, 1923.

Dempsey, Dave. *On the Brink: The Great Lakes in the 21st Century.* East Lansing: Michigan State University Press, 2004.

DeSantis, Tom. *Niagara's Parks: International Stewardship from an Ecological Perspective* (unpublished master's thesis). Buffalo: School of Architecture and Planning, SUNY Buffalo, 1996.

DiNunzio, Michael G. *Adirondack Wildguide: A Natural History of the Adirondack Park*. Keene Valley, NY: Adirondack Nature Conservancy, 1984.

Doty, Lockwood L. *A History of Livingston County New York*. Republished from the original 1876 edition: Geneseo: Livingston County Historian, 1979.

Driscoll, Charles et al. *Acid Rain Revisited: Advances in Scientific Understanding Since the Passage of the 1970 and 1990 Clean Air Act Amendments*. Hanover, NH: Hubbard Brook Research Foundation, Science Links Publication, Vol. 1, No. 1.

Emoto, Masaru. *Messages from Water*. www.hadousa.com.

Engelbrecht, William. *Iroquoia: The Development of a Native World*. Syracuse: Syracuse University Press, 2003.

Environmental Defence and Canadian Environmental Law Association. *Partners in Pollution*. Toronto: CELA, 2006.

Fiske, John. *New France and New England*. Boston: Houghton, Mifflin, 1902.

Fitzpatrick, John C., editor. *The Writings of George Washington*, Vol. 15. Washington, DC: U.S. Government Printing Office, 1936.

Gateley, Susan Peterson. *The Great Atomic Lake: Energy Policy, Security, and Nuclear Power on Lake Ontario*. New York: published by the author, 2002.

Great Lakes Fishery Commission. "Lake Ontario Committee." www.glfc.org.

Great Lakes United. *Citizens Speak*. Buffalo: Great Lakes United, 1999.

Grinde, Donald A., and Bruce E. Johansen. *Exemplar of Liberty: Native America and the Evolution of Democracy*. Los Angeles: University of California Press, 1991.

———. *Ecocide of Native America: Environmental Destruction of Indian Lands and People*. Santa Fe: Clear Light Publishers, 1995.

Haudenosaunee Environmental Task Force. *Words that Come Before All Else*. Akwesasne, Ontario: Native North American Travelling College, 1999.

Hauptman, Laurence M. *The Iroquois Struggle for Survival*. Syracuse: Syracuse University Press, 1986.

Hawthorne, Nathaniel. "My Visit to Niagara" in *Nathaniel Hawthorne: Tales and Sketches*. New York: Library of America, 1982.

Hennepin, Louis. *"New Discovery of a Vast Country in America."* London: M. Bentley, 1698.

Herman Leroy Fairchild. *Geologic Story of the Genesee Valley and Western New York*. Rochester, NY: published by the author, 1928.

Houghton, Frederick. "History of the Buffalo Creek Reservation," *Buffalo Historical Society Publications*, Vol. XXIV. Buffalo: Buffalo Historical Society, 1920.

Hunt, David M. et al. *Lake Erie Gorges: Biodiversity Inventory and Landscape Integrity Analyis.* Albany: New York Natural Heritage Program, October 2002.

International Joint Commission. *Revised Great Lakes Water Quality Agreement of 1978.* Ottawa and Washington, DC: International Joint Commission, February 1994.

————. *Sixth Biennial Report on Great Lakes Water Quality.* Washington, DC, Ottawa, and Windsor: IJC, 1992.

Irvine, K. N. et al. *Assessment of Potential Aquatic Habitat Restoration Sites in the Buffalo River Area of Concern.* Buffalo: Buffalo State SUNY, 2005.

Jackson, Wes. 'Toward an Ignorance-based Worldview," in *The Land Report.* Salina: The Land Institute, Spring 2005, No. 81.

LaBastille, Anne. *Beyond Black Bear Lake.* New York: W.W. Norton, 1987.

Lane, Christopher W. *Impressions of Niagara.* Philadelphia: Philadelphia Print Shop, 1993.

Laub, Richard S., editor. *The Hiscock Site.* Buffalo Society of Natural Sciences Bulletin, Vol. 27, Buffalo, 1975.

League of Women Voters, "Education Campaign on Urban Sprawl," www.lwvbn.org/sprawl/.

Leopold, Aldo. *A Sand County Almanac and Sketches Here and There.* London: Oxford University Press, 1949.

————. *The River of the Mother of God and Other Essays.* Edited by Susan L. Flader and J. Baird Callicott. Madison: University of Wisconsin Press, 1991.

Lewandowski, Stephen. *One Life.* St. Albans, VT: Wood Thrush Books, 2001.

Marshall, Orasmus H. "The Niagara Frontier," *Publications of the Buffalo Historical Society,* Vol. II. Buffalo: Bigelow Brothers, 1880.

May, Herbert, and Bruce Metzger, editors. *The Oxford Annotated Bible with the Apocrypha.* New York: Oxford University Press, 1962.

McCausland, Walter. "The People of Seneca Indian Park," *Niagara Frontier,* Winter 1963, Vol. 9, No. 4.

McHarg, Ian. *Design with Nature.* Garden City: Doubleday, 1971.

McKibben, Bill. *Hope, Human and Wild.* Little, Brown, 1996.

Meyer, Judy L. et al. *Where Rivers Are Born: The Scientific Imperative for Defending Small Streams and Watersheds.* Athens, GA: American Rivers and Sierra Club, 2003.

Michalenko, Edward, editor. *The State of Onondaga Lake.* Syracuse: Onondaga Lake Cleanup Corp., 2001.

Mitchell, Kerry. *Pathway to Peace: What Heritage Based Collaboration Offers the Cross-Border Niagara Region.* Buffalo: Canadian Consulate General, 2004.

Neruda, Pablo. *The Book of Questions.* Port Townsend, WA: Copper Canyon Press, 1991.

New York Power Authority. "Final Report: Historic Presence and Current Status of Atlantic Salmon in the St. Lawrence River and Lake Ontario," 2004.

New York State Canal Corporation. *A Report on the Future of New York State Canals,* December 2005. www.canals.state.ny.us.

New York State Department of Environmental Conservation. *Oswego River RAP: Stage 3—Delisting.* Albany: NYSDEC, May 2002.

New York State Department of Environmental Conservation. *Contaminants in Young-of-Year Fish from Selected Lake Ontario Tributaries.* Albany: NYSDEC, December 1988.

New York State Department of Environmental Conservation. *New York State Hazardous Waste Facility Siting Plan.* Albany: NYSDEC, 2000.

Norton, Bryan G. *Sustainability: A Philosophy of Adaptive Ecosystem Management.* Chicago: University of Chicago Press, 2005.

Olmsted, Frederick Law. *General Plan for the Improvement of the Niagara Reservation.* Niagara Falls, NY: Gazette Book and Job Office, 1887.

Outwater, Alice. *Water: A Natural History.* New York: Basic Books, 1996.

Parker, Arthur C. *Seneca Myths and Folk Tales.* Lincoln: University of Nebraska Press, 1989.

———. *The Life of General Ely S. Parker.* Buffalo: Buffalo Historical Society, 1919.

Pedersen, Gilbert J. "Early Title to Indian Reservations in Western New York," *Niagara Frontier,* Vol. 3, 1956–1957.

Pennsylvania Transportation Institute. *Analysis of the Great Lakes/St. Lawrence River Navigation System's Role in U.S. Ocean Container Trade.* University Park: Pennsylvania State University, August 2003.

Rostlund, Erhard. *Freshwater Fish and Fishing in Native North America.* Berkeley: University of California Press, 1952.

Roy, Arudhati. "The Greater Common Good" at www.narmada.org/gcg/gcg.html.

Russell, Eber. *Collected Papers.* The Patterson Library, 40 South Portage Street, Westfield, NY, 14787.

Sauer, David E. *An Environmental History of the Buffalo River.* Buffalo: Buffalo Color Corporation, 1990.

Schneekloth, Lynda, and Margaret Wooster. "Imagining Buffalo: Stories and Reflections," in *Urban Resources,* Vol. 1, No. 4, Spring 1984.

Sever, James E., editor. *A Narrative of the Life of Mrs. Mary Jemison.* Syracuse: Syracuse University Press, 1990.

Severance, Frank. *An Old Frontier of France,* Vol. 1. New York: Dodd Mead, 1918.

Shenandoah, Joanne, and Douglas M. George. *Skywoman: Legends of the Iroquois.* Santa Fe: Clear Light Publishers, 1998.

Shongo, Moses. "Indian Papers" Box 1, Folder 15, no date. Buffalo Historical Society research library.

Slade, John. *Acid Rain, Acid Snow.* New York: Woodgate International, 2000.

Spitzer, Eliot. Submission and comments, May 1, 2003. www.oag.state. ny.us/press/statements.

Stafford, J. A., and J. V. Ward. "An Ecosystem Perspective on Alluvial Rivers," in *Journal of the American Benthological Society,* Vol. 12, 1993.

Tesmer, Irving H. *Geology of Cattaraugus County.* Buffalo Society of Natural Sciences Bulletin, Vol. 27, Buffalo, 1975.

Traven, B. *The Treasure of the Sierra Madre.* New York: Noonday Press, 1935.

U.S. Environmental Protection Agency and Envirnment Canada. *State of the Great Lakes 2007, Highlights Report.* www.epa.gov/glnpo/solec/sogl,2007.

U.S. Fish and Wildlife Service. "A Wealth of Wildlife: New Breed of Tourism Fuels North Forest Economy," *AMC Outdoors Magazine,* June 2004.

U.S. Fish and Wildlife Service. *American Eel Status Review Workshop 1.* November 19–December 1, 2005, Sheperdstown, West Virginia. www.fws.gov/ northeast/ameel/.

U.S. Geological Survey, Great Lakes Science Center. "Zebra Mussels Cause Economic and Ecological Harm in the Great Lakes." www.glsc.usgs.gov/- files/factsheets.

Vaughan, Ray et al. *Geology Reports.* East Concord, NY: Coalition on West Valley Nuclear Wastes, 1994.

Vollman, William T. *Fathers and Crows, Volume II of Seven Dreams: A Book of North American Landscapes.* New York: Viking, 1992.

Wallace, Paul A. W. *The White Roots of Peace.* Saranac Lake: Chauncy Press, 1986.

Wilson, James. *The Earth Shall Weep: A History of Native America.* New York: Atlantic Monthly Press, 1998.

Wooster, Margaret. *Bioregionalism and Environmental Planning* (unpublished master's thesis). Buffalo: School of Architecture and Planning, SUNY Buffalo, 1988.

INDEX

acid rain, 113–19, 186, 190
adaptive management, 84, 185
Adirondack Council, 117
Adirondack Mountains: xi, 109–23, 144, 145, 151, 152, 164, 186; acid rain, 113–19; beaver, 120–22; fish, 111–16, 118; and Great Lakes, 109–10; map of, 108
Akwesasne, 145–46, 188
Akzo Salt Inc., 81–84, 185
Allegheny River: glacial history, 95–96; Kinzua Dam, 27; and Seneca, 57
Allen, Ahaz, 89, 90, 102
American eel: map of range, 129; and Oswego River, 127–29, 132; and Sargasso Sea, 127–29; and St. Lawrence River, 142, 159, 163, 186–87
aquifers, 11, 43, 83, 90–91
Atlantic salmon: map of range, 131; and Onondaga Lake, 137; and Oswego River, 127, 130–32; 135; and St. Lawrence River, 130–32, 142, 163, 187

bald eagle: and DDT, 6,8; and Endangered Species Act, 132–33; return of, 132–33, 179
Beauharnois Dam, 162–63
beaver: Adirondack, 120–22; Buffalo River, 53–54; Scajaquada Creek, 36, 37, 40, 48

bioregionalism, xv, 193
Berg, Peter, xii
Berry, Wendell, xii, 84, 103, 185
Big Tree Treaty, 55, 79, 89
Black Rock, 36–39
botulism, 43, 144, 173
Boundary Waters Treaty, 7, 22–23, 142
Buffalo Color, 52, 61–63, 68, 184
Buffalo Niagara Riverkeeper, ix, 28, 65–67
Buffalo River: 51–69; early inhabitants, 53–58; fish, 53; grain elevators, 52, 55, 58–60; industrial history, 52–53, 61–63; map of AOC, 50; River Rats, 68–69
Burton Act, 23, 25
Bush, George W., 117

Caldarelli, Dawn, 62
Canadian Auto Workers, 176
Canadian Environmental Protection Act, 7, 176–77
Cartier, Jacques: 131, 136, 143–44, 148; boulevard and mall, 167; mountain, 166; museum, 167; voyages, 141, 149–50, 152–56, 159–62, 187
Cattaraugus Creek: xi, 87–105; aquifer, 90–91; geology, 95–98, 185; and Haudenosaunee, 57, 87, 92–94, 96, 100; map of 86; West Valley nuclear waste, 89, 96–100

ABOUT THE AUTHOR

MARGARET WOOSTER is the author of *Somewhere to Go on Sunday: A Guide to Natural Treasures in Western New York and Southern Ontario.* Her essays on urban rivers have appeared in *Art Voice, Buffalo Spree, Urban Resources, New York Folklore,* and *Western New York Heritage.* She has worked for river and creek preservation as a watershed planner for local and county governments in western New York and as the executive director of a binational Great Lakes advocacy coalition, Great Lakes United. She is currently completing a river-based habitat assessment for Buffalo Niagara Riverkeeper, a not-for-profit organization that uses legal, scientific, and policy tools on behalf of the Niagara river bio-region. Margaret lives with her family on the Onondaga Escarpment in Buffalo New York.